CW00520318

RECIPE

**THE WORLD WENT INTO LOCKDOWN,
WE WENT INTO THE KITCHEN**

Editors: Roberto Chiesa & Paul Cooper

First Published by Clan Destine Press in 2022
PO Box 121, Bittern
Victoria, Australia
www.clandestinepress.net

Clan Destine
PRESS

ISBN: 9781922904195

Cover Design and internal layout by the team at Dinosaurus.

TABLE OF CONTENTS
What's where

TABLE OF CONTENTS
(continued)

MEASUREMENT CONVERSIONS
A handy conversion table

Cups	Grams	Ounces	Millilitres
¼ cup	32 g	1 ⅛ oz	32 ml
½ cup	64 g	2 ¼ oz	64 ml
⅔ cup	85 g	3 oz	85 ml
¾ cup	96 g	3 ⅓ oz	96 ml
1 cup	128 g	4.5 oz	128 ml

INTRODUCTION

ROBERTO CHIESA,
APRIL, 2022

As the pandemic took hold and major airlines were cancelling flights, our travel industry was one of the first affected by the coronavirus. On March 23, 2020 I set up a Facebook group called "Our Home Made Recipes in the Time of COVID-19".

I did not for a moment imagine that it was going to become such a popular group. We are a family of passionate tourism and travel people from all over the world who are mostly connected to Australia, New Zealand and the Pacific Ocean. These regions are far from Europe and North America, but 'Down Under' is the area we have chosen to promote to our clients.

I honestly do not remember how I got the idea but from the very first Facebook group post our tourism and travel "family" responded positively with the usual load of passion and friendship that has always distinguished all of us.

The kitchen is a place where family come together, to cook and sit together and enjoy a meal. When we travel, we dine at great restaurants and chat about life over fine food and wine together. But world wide lock downs took this simple pleasure away. However this Facebook cooking group allowed us to gather just like in real life and at times allowed us to connect with lost friends, to joke, to have fun and do serious conversations. The rest, as they say, is history.

We did not need any group rules or post expectations, our long-term travel family just continued our great bond in an online environment. By February 2021, just 12 months after starting the group, over 600 travel and tourism industry colleagues and friends had posted over 4,500 times attracting 16,000 comments and 21,000 reactions of creative cooking ideas and recipe sharing from their home kitchens.

Our group is made up of company directors, product managers, tourism operators and suppliers, booking agents, reservations staff and more. But none are professional chefs! Our written recipes, description of them and the photographs are from our home kitchens and they are made with love, irony and creativity for those who are close and for those who are far.

These recipes were a simple way to stay connected and to keep our relationships solid during the toughest time the travel industry has ever faced. We never lost heart, we are resilient and we are already looking at the future as we have always done.

If these are just some of the recipes made at home in kitchens around the world, just imagine the joys of taking your taste buds back on holidays as the world is once more yours to discover. We are ready to show you first hand why we are so passionate about travel.

Bon appétit
Roberto Chiesa
Product Manager and Partner
Go Australia
Italy

FOREWORD

PAUL COOPER,
APRIL, 2022

To see just some of the thousands of recipes from our online group live in a book is not only an ongoing reminder of how we all stuck together during these tough times, but it will also be a book to share, enjoy and re-live the joys we were able to get from such a wonderful and resilient tourism industry family.

As an Australian tourism supplier, the support that we get when selling Australia and our road trips in particular continues to go from strength to strength.

Personally, I have enjoyed awesome friendships and wonderful support from the travel industry and it is an honour to put a little bit back by assisting with the production of this book.

I hope you get some time in the kitchen to explore these home made recipes and then share them with family and friends.

Paul Cooper
Marketing and Business Development Manager
Sydney-Melbourne Touring
Australia

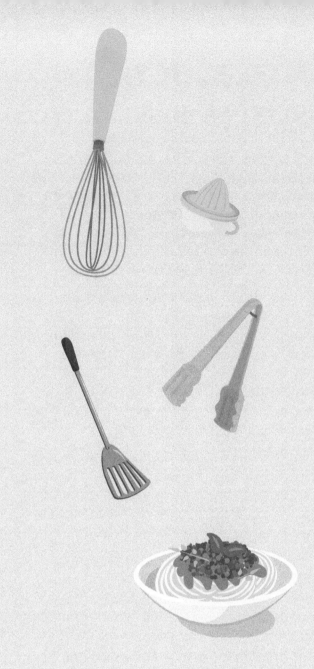

CONTRIBUTORS

Our recipes do not follow a strict order especially because we come from all over the globe.

CONTRIBUTORS COME FROM:

Australia • Austria • Belgium • Brazil • Canada • Chile • United Arab Emirates • Fiji
Philippines • Finland • France • French Polynesia • Germany • Greece • Hong Kong
Cook Islands • Italy • Jersey • Malaysia • Norway • New Zealand • Netherlands
Papua New Guinea • Poland • United Kingdom • Samoa • Singapore • Slovenia • Spain
United States of America • South Africa • Sweden • Switzerland • Vietnam

FIRST DISHES / STARTERS

RACLETTE

Serves 2+

INGREDIENTS / ELEMENTS

Raclette Oven / Griller
Small cooked potatoes
Any vegetables: sweet corn, gherkins,
tomatoes, mushrooms, capsicums, onions
Meat/seafood: ham, salami, prawns, tuna
Fruit: pears, apples
Raclette cheese
(or any other types of good melting cheeses:
Gorgonzola, Cheddar, Gouda, goat cheese)
Green salad
Baguettes

TIPS

1) If serving potatoes cook them beforehand.
2) Most vegetables cook easily in the raclette.

THE COOK

Eva Seller
Frankfurt, Germany

**Regional General Mgr
– Continental Europe:**
Tourism Australia

METHOD / DESCRIPTION

Preparation

A Raclette dinner/meal is the easiest lunch, dinner or impromptu grazing experience ever.
It is ideal for two people, a family or many guests. It is both simple and elegant – ideal for casual
meals or fancy dinner parties. Raclette is both the name of a cheese and the grill on which it is
fried or melted. The experience is a little like a fondue except instead of dipping food into cheese,
the cheese is melted and poured or spread over the foods on your plate. And those foods,
whether vegetables, fruit or meats, are cooked by your guests at the table on the raclette.
Raclette is a great way to empty the fridge of all kinds of leftover food or things that won't
stretch to a meal by themselves. Or you can buy any favourite foods that go well with melted
cheese. It's also an ideal way to cater for different dietary requirements or food preferences
as everybody chooses and cooks their own. The only real preparation is dicing the foods into
small pieces so that they fit into the small raclette frying pans.
Raclette is a beautifully sociable dinner that can go on for a long time.

FUGASSIN (POTATO BUNS)

Serves 4

INGREDIENTS

500 g potatoes
500 g flour
1 cube brewer's yeast
(alternatively, use freeze-dried yeast
for savory pies)
Oil for frying

THE COOK

Roberto Chiesa
Torino, Italy

Tour Operator and GM:
Go Australia

TIPS

1) Fugassin are a tasty snack.
2) An ideal accompaniment to your favourite meat dish.

METHOD

Preparation
Boil potatoes. Once cooked and warm, peel potatoes and mash with a fork or a potato masher.
Add flour and knead. Dissolve yeast in a little warm water, add to the dough and continue
to knead until mixture is soft. Leave to rise for about two hours. Cut dough into small pieces
of approximately 8-10 cm and gently press them until you obtain donuts of about 6-8 cm.
I recommend you add flour to flattened dough to prevent mixture from sticking.

The Cooking
Heat at least half a litre of oil (or use a deep fryer). When the oil is hot, immerse potato pancakes
one by one and let them fry until they swell and turn golden brown.

The Finale
Drain oil from the buns on paper towel and sprinkle with grated Parmesan cheese.

TORTELLINI SALAD

Serves 2

INGREDIENTS

250 g tortellini pasta
150 g yoghurt
1-2 spoons of mayonnaise
2 slices of Gouda
2 slices of ham
1/2 cucumber
1 tomato
2-3 garlic cloves
Salt, pepper and dukkah

TIP

A very easy recipe which tastes even better if you prepare it the day before your party or get-together.

THE COOK

Inka van Baal
Germany

Product and Marketing Manager:
Best of Travel Group

METHOD

The Pasta
Cook tortellini in plenty of salted water.

Preparation
Slice cucumber in little cubes and tomato into little boats. Dice Gouda and ham into little bits. Crush or dice garlic.

The Sauce
Mix yoghurt and mayonnaise together in a large bowl. Add garlic, cucumber, tomato, Gouda and ham and mix well. Season with salt and pepper and add some dukkah. Alternativley, use chilli pepper or wasabi to add a bit of heat.

The Finale
Finally, add the boiled tortellini, stir through the sauce and serve.

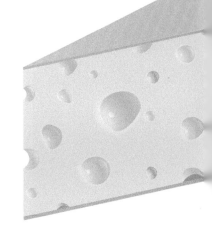

SALMON AND MANGO TERRINE

Serves 8

INGREDIENTS

800 g salmon (no skin, no bones)
1 lime
1 tbsp grated fresh ginger
2 egg whites
1 mango
2 leeks
200 ml full cream (liquid)
Coriander (according to taste)
Basil
Salt and pepper

THE COOK

Aurelia Devilliers-Fezay
Villemomble, France

Product Manager:
Australie Tours

> **TIP**
> Put baking paper in the mould to make
> it easier to remove the terrine when cooked.

METHOD

Preparation
Pre-heat the oven to 120° C. Grate the zest of the lime. Separate egg whites.
Peel and cut mango into strips and sprinkle them with lemon juice. Cut 250 g of salmon into cubes and the remaining salmon into large strips, then place in fridge for 15 minutes.

The Salmon
Mix the salmon cubes with the zest, ginger and 2 egg whites. Add the cream, stirring constantly. Season with salt and pepper. Season the salmon strips with salt, pepper and chopped basil.

The Leeks
Clean the leeks and keep the longest leaves. Cook them in boiling water for one minute, then dip them into ice water. Drain and pat them dry.

The Terrine
Cover base and sides of a buttered cake mould with leek leaves, leaving the ends out.
Layer mould with ginger salmon mix, then salmon strips, then mango and repeat until all ingredients are used. Finish with a layer of ginger salmon. Fold ends of leek leaves over contents of the terrine. Bake in the oven for 50 to 60 minutes.

The Finale
Remove and allow to cool. Decorate with coriander and set aside in fridge to chill. Serve in slices.

PIZZA MARGHERITA WITH QUICK BASE

Serves 2

INGREDIENTS

29 cm pizza pan

The Dough
63 g quark (soft cheese)
50 ml milk
25 ml olive oil
125 g flour
1/2 tsp salt
4 g baking powder

Margherita Topping
400 g fresh tomatoes (or 1 tin chopped)
Tomato purée
150 g mozzarella
Basil and oregano
Olive oil

THE COOK

Karin Marty
Zurich, Switzerland

Oceania Product Manager:
Travelhouse

TIP

1) Use the same base to make a tarte flambée by topping it with sour cream, bacon and onion.

METHOD

The Base
Mix 25 ml of olive oil, 50 ml of milk and the quark with a whisk. Add half of the flour, a pinch of salt and the baking powder. Mix well using a spoon, then add remaining flour.
Knead mixture until you have a nice dough. Let dough rest for 30 minutes in a covered bowl in fridge. Then roll dough out very thinly and place on the pan.

The Topping
Pre-heat oven to 250° C. Cut mozzarella into thin slices and drain canned tomatoes.
Spread tomato purée thinly over base, leaving an outer edge. Spread base with diced tomato pieces, then mozzarella. Sprinkle your favourite herbs, basil, oregano etc. and splash a few drops of olive oil over it.

The Cooking
Bake on middle rack of oven for around seven minutes.

The Finale
Watch your pizza as it cooks. Depending on your oven, it could cook quickly.

SPAGHETTI EGG TWIST

Serves 4

INGREDIENTS

350 g spaghetti
4 eggs
Anchovies in oil
Chives
Chilli
100 g breadcrumbs
1 garlic clove
Salt
100 ml extra virgin olive oil

TIPS

1) Spaghetti must be al dente.
2) Add a few spoons of oil while the spaghetti is cooking.
3) Leave out anchovies if not to your taste.

THE COOK

Carmen Laurella
Italy
Sales Manager UK/Europe:
Luxury Hotels Australia

METHOD

The Pasta
Boil water with salt and cook pasta. Add a few teaspoons of olive oil so spaghetti does not stick together. It will stilll require a bit of stirring. When cooked al dente, drain the pasta.

The Sauce
Heat 100 ml of olive oil and garlic in a pan. Add breadcrumbs and cook until brown. Stir frequently.

The Eggs
Fry the eggs in a separate pan.

The Finale
Add cooked spaghetti to pan with breadcrumbs and mix well. Serve on plates with fried egg on top. Sprinkle with some chilli, chopped chives and a few anchovies. Enjoy!

SPAGHETTI SALSICCIA RAGOUT

Serves 2

INGREDIENTS

500 g salsiccia peperoncino
1 onion
1 garlic clove
350 g cherry tomatoes
3 tbsp olive oil
Salt and pepper
2 bay leaves
1 sprig of rosemary
500 ml strained, tinned tomatoes
1 bunch of parsley
500 g spaghetti

THE COOK

Sabine Schamburger
Trier, Germany

Product Manager:
Boomerang Reisen

" Salsiccia is an Italian coarse-grain raw sausage, similar to the coarse German bratwurst, in structure and basic taste. But salsiccia uses different herbs like sage, coriander, fennel, cilantro, and garlic, depending on the region. "

TIP

If salsiccia is not available, use any other type of coarse minced sausage meat, and season it with chilli and other herbs and spices while frying.

METHOD

Preparation
Peel salsiccia and form into small balls. Finely dice onion and garlic. Wash and halve tomatoes. Wash parsley, shake dry and chop.

The Pasta
Cook spaghetti al dente, then drain.

The Ragout
Heat oil in pot and briefly sauté onions and garlic. Add salsiccia balls and sauté. Season with salt and pepper. Add bay leaves, rosemary sprig, cherry and strained tomatoes and simmer ragout for about 45 minutes on low heat.

The Finale
Mix cooked spaghetti with ragout. Serve with parsley.

SPRINGTIME LASAGNE WITH VEGETABLES

Serves 4

INGREDIENTS

180 g egg lasagna
800 g cherry tomatoes
500 g asparagus
200 g courgette (zucchini)
200 g aubergine (eggplant)
125 g pickled black olives
200 g snow peas or green beans
75 g Fontal/Fontina cheese
(provolone as a substitute)
75 g minced mozzarella
75 g grated Provolone cheese
50 g grated Parmesan
50 g grated Emmentaler
6 anchovies fillets in oil
1 garlic clove
30 g zucchini flowers
3 basil leaves
Salt and black pepper
Extra virgin olive oil
Baking pan 30 x 20 cm
Asparagus tips

For the fondue
500 g whole milk
250 g Fontal cheese
Nutmeg to taste

MAKING THE FONDUE

Chop Fontal cheese into cubes. Warm milk in a saucepan, when it starts to boil, turn off the heat and add Fontal. Mix with a whisk until cheese is melted. Flavour with a little nutmeg. Fondue will be ready once sauce is smooth and without lumps.

THE COOK

Sabrina Sicura
Ancona, Italy

Booking: Go Australia

METHOD

Preparation
Cut pitted olives into rings and cherry tomatoes in half. Crush garlic. Tear basil leaves. Thinly slice aubergines and courgettes, lengthwise. Wash and dry courgette flowers and gently remove stem and pistils.

Pre-cooking the vegetables
Stand asparagus stems in asparagus pot with tips out of the water and cook for a few minutes. Drain while still crunchy, allow to cool then dice stems. Leave tips whole and put aside for final layer. Grill aubergine and courgette pieces for a few minutes on each side. Steam snow peas, leaving them crunchy. Grate Parmesan, Emmentaler, Provolone and mozzarella and mix together.

The Sautéed Vegetable Sauce
Heat a little olive oil in large pan, add drained anchovy fillets and garlic. Melt over low heat. Add olives, basil, asparagus stems and cherry tomatoes. Raise heat a little. Add snow peas, Salt and pepper to taste. Turn off after two minutes.

Building the Lasagne
Brush bottom of baking tray with olive oil, cover with lasagna sheets then a layer of sauce. Top with grilled zucchini and aubergines, cover with Fontal fondue, then a spread of mixed grated cheese. Repeat layers twice. Decorate with mixed cheese, asparagus and courgette flowers.

The Finale
Bake the lasagna in a preheated oven at 180° C for 35 minutes and serve.

SUMMER COLOURS PASTA

Serves 3

INGREDIENTS

5 capsicums
5 red onions
20 pickled black olives
20-30 capers
Olive oil
Breadcrumbs
Strozzapretti or trofie pasta

THE COOK

Mario Cascione
Italy

Tourism Software House:
Travelidea

METHOD

Preparation
Dice all the vegetables.

The Pasta
Cook pasta in lots of salted boiling water. Drain when al dente and set aside.

The Cooking
Heat olive oil in a pan, add vegetables and cook for 20 minutes.
In another pan warm some olive oil, add breadcrumbs and fry for one minute.

The Finale
Stir cooked pasta into vegetables and mix well.
Serve in bowls and sprinkle with fried breadcrumbs.

WHOLEMEAL SPAGHETTI WITH ANCHOVIES

Serves 4

INGREDIENTS

350 g wholemeal spaghetti
16 anchovy fillets in oil
80 g salted capers
3 tbsp of extra virgin olive oil
(for a more intense flavour you can also use
the anchovy oil)
2-3 garlic cloves
150 g pickled Taggiasca olives (black)
70 g pine nuts
(Stale) breadcrumbs
Salt and freshly ground pepper
Optional: wild fennel or finely chopped parsley

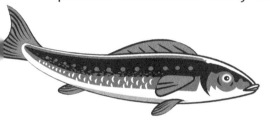

THE COOK

Antonella Valerio
Torino, Italy
Booking: Go Asia

METHOD

Preparation
Desalt capers in cold water, then drain and dry them. Lightly toast pine nuts and breadcrumbs.

The Pasta
Cook spaghetti al dente in plenty of boiling salted water, then drain.

The Sauce
Heat 3 tbsp of olive oil in a wok pan and brown garlic cloves whole.
Mix in olives, capers and pepper. Remove garlic. Add anchovies. Pound them with a wooden spoon until they dissolve in the oil. The sauce is ready.

The Finale
Add cooked spaghetti to anchovy sauce and mix well.
Transfer to a serving dish or pasta bowls.
Sprinkle with toasted pine nuts and breadcrumbs,
pepper and (optional) fennel or parsley.

STRAMMER MAX PLUS

Serves 1

INGREDIENTS

1-2 slices of your favourite bread
Butter or avocado
Gouda, goat's cheese or your favourite cheese
Slices of ham
Antipasto veggies or veggies in aspic
2-3 eggs
Olive oil
Salt, pepper and favourite herbs
Ketchup
Curry powder
Cherry (cocktail) tomatoes
Mini gherkins

THE COOK

Inka van Baal
Germany

**Product and
Marketing Manager:**
Best of Travel Group

TIPS

1) A radler is the perfect drink to pair with a Strammer Max.
2) A radler – known in some places as a shandy – is beer mixed with lemonade.

" *A Strammer Max is an open-faced sandwich. The traditional Berlin version is a slice of bread – sometimes fried in butter – topped with ham and egg. My version has a few sug gested and delicious extras.* "

METHOD

Preparation
Slice mini gherkins and cherry tomatoes for each plate as sides or for decoration. Slice cheese and ham – not too thick.
Choose one or two slices of your favourite bread and butter it or spread with avocado.

To Fry or Not to Fry
You can, if you like, fry bread in butter or oil. Or leave cold.

First Layers
Layer bread with preferred cheese and slices of ham.
Add slice of veggies in aspic or sundried tomatoes or other antipasto-type vegetables.

The Finale
Fry 2 or 3 eggs, season with salt, pepper and favourite herbs.
Add to the stack on your bread.

MOULES AU CIDRE ET AUX LARDONS

Serves 2-4

INGREDIENTS

2 kg of fresh moules (mussels)
Can or bottle of your favourite cider
1 large onion
1 garlic clove
200 g bacon lardons or streaky bacon
60 g butter
Full fat crème fraiche or double cream
Parsley
Crusty bread to serve

THE COOK

Susie De Carteret
Jersey, Channel Islands, UK

Sales and Promotion:
Tasmanian Odyssey

TIPS

1) You can use white wine, but we cook the Moules in cider, along a spoonful of crème fraiche or cream. It makes a richer, rounder dish. I use local Jersey cider but any will do.
2) When in season, we also serve with a dish of delicious Jersey Royal Potatoes dripping in butter for pure gluttony.

❝ Moules (or mussels) are a popular Jersey dish for most of the year and are a favourite in our family. Our Moules are smaller and sweeter than the Scottish variety usually served in the UK. Moules au Cidre et aux Lardons reflects Jersey's proximity to the French coasts of Brittany and Normandy, the closest place being the little town of Carteret in Normandy, which can easily be seen from our east coast. And Carteret was where my husband's family (de Carteret) originally came from, way back in the 11th Century! ❞

METHOD

Preparation

Rinse moules in cold water.
Discard any that are broken or don't close when tapped hard. Finely chop onion, garlic and handful of parsley. Dice bacon.

The Sauce

Melt butter in a large pan. Gently sauté lardons, garlic and onions until latter is soft and lightly coloured. Pour in most of the can of cider (300 ml) and bring to the boil. Drink the rest!

The Cooking

Tip moules into sauce, cover with a tight fitting lid and cook over medium-high heat, shaking pan occasionally, for about 4 minutes – or until shells have opened. Remove moules with a slotted spoon and keep warm, discarding any still tightly closed. Reduce sauce quickly over high heat and add a tbsp of crème fraiche or cream to taste, cooking gently until combined.

The Finale

Season with salt and pepper. Share moules into bowls and pour the sauce over each.
Serve with warm crusty bread to mop up sauce. Prepare to get messy and dive in!

SOLES A L'OSTENDAISE

Serves 2

INGREDIENTS

2 pieces of sole
2 kg mussels
500 g deshelled Flemish grey shrimps
10 ml freshly squeezed lemon juice
40 ml dry white wine
1 bouquet garni
20 ml cream
200 g butter
1 egg yolk
Potatoes, butter and milk for mash

" *Enjoy one of the treasures of the North Sea. Ostend sole is a great dish to make at home.* "

THE COOK

Marc A. Lambert
Bruxelles, Belgique

Consultant:
Qvo Vadis Tourism

TIPS

1) Keep the cooking liquids (stock) from the sole and mussels to use in the sauce.
2) Mashed potato is the perfect accompaniment to this dish.

METHOD

The Sole
Arrange ready-to-cook sole in large greased oven dish. Season with salt and pepper and cover with lemon juice and white wine.
Add bouquet garni and cover with sheet of greased kitchen paper.
Poach in medium hot oven until done. Keep warm when cooked.

The Mussels
Cook the mussels in boiling water for about four minutes then remove them from their shells. Keep liquid. Remove fish from oven dish. Use sieve to collect liquid.

The Sauce
Pour sieved mussel stock and liquid from mussels into a small pan. Add cream, bring to a simmer and allow to thicken. Beat egg yolk in some lemon juice. Add the mussels and shrimps to the sauce and thicken further by adding egg yolk. Remove from hob and stir in some knobs of ice-cold butter

The Finale
Arrange warm sole on hot plates and cover in sauce.
Serve with mashed potato.

STEAMED MUSSELS WITH BLACK BEAN SAUCE

Serves 2

INGREDIENTS

1 kg black mussels
5-6 garlic cloves
Fresh ginger
3 birds eye chillies
1 bunch of spring onions
Black bean sauce
Soy sauce
Shaoxing cooking wine
Cooking oil
Corn flour

THE COOK

Feng Tam
Adelaide, Australia

Owner:
Respiratory PhysiO2

METHOD

Preparation
Rinse mussels. Finely chop garlic. Grate thumb-size knob of ginger. Dice chillies and spring onions.

The Sauce
Heat oil in deep pan on high heat. Stir fry ginger, garlic, chilli and spring onion for a couple of minutes. Add 3 tbsp of black bean sauce and stir till fragrant, around 2 minutes.
Add 1 tbsp soy sauce, 1 cup cooking wine and mix well. Add 1 tbsp corn flour to 50 ml cold water and mix well. Slowly add cornflour water to sauce and mix well to thicken it.

The Mussels
Add mussels to sauce, cover with lid and steam for 5 min.
The mussels are done when shells open. (Don't overcook them, they will shrink.)

The Finale
Serve with your favourite side dishes.

STEAMED PRAWNS WITH MUNG BEAN VERMICELLI

Serves 4-6

INGREDIENTS

10-20 large whole prawns with shells
1 packet of mung bean vermicelli
2-3 garlic cloves
Soy sauce
Sugar
Cooking oil

THE COOK

Feng Tam
Adelaide, Australia

Owner:
Respiratory PhysiO2

METHOD

Preparation
Dice or mince garlic. Dice spring onions. De-vein prawns and slice along their backs to open them up. Fill the open backs of each prawn with garlic.

The Prawns and The Vermicelli
Bring water in a steamer to the boil. Add prawns and steam for 6 minutes. Meanwhile, bring a small saucepan of water to the boil, add vermicelli and cook for 5 minutes. Drain and spread on a deep serving plate. Remove the cooked prawns from the steamer and arrange on top of the vermicelli.

The Sauce
Heat half a cup of cooking oil in small saucepan then pour evenly over prawns.
In the same saucepan bring 3 tbsp soy sauce, 1 tsp sugar and half cup of water to the boil for 1 minute, stirring well. Pour sauce evenly over prawns and vermicelli.

The Finale
Garnish prawns with diced spring onion. Serve.

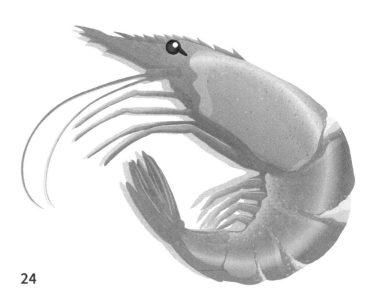

BEST PIZZA EVER

Serves 2-4

INGREDIENTS

Dough
950 g of white flour
50 g of corn flour
800 ml of water
2 tbsp of mother yeast
4 tsp of honey
Salt
A cup of oil
Cling film

TOPPINGS

Anything you like!
Suggestions: sliced onion, ham, artichoke hearts, sun-dried capsicum, tomato, olives, anchovies, mozarella cheese, capers, bacon.

THE COOK

Sabrina Sicura
Ancona, Italy

Booking: Go Australia

TIPS

1) This dough needs to be prepared two days before you want to make your pizza.
2) You will need containers for helping the dough rise and trays for cooking the pizza bases.

METHOD

The Dough
Use a fork to mix flour, corn flour, yeast, water and honey in a bowl. When well mixed, add 1.5 tsps of salt and a cup of oil. Knead dough until thoroughly mixed.
Wrap dough in cling film then place in a container in fridge. Leave pizza dough to rest in the fridge for 12 hours. Remove from the fridge and let the dough rise at room temperature for 18 hours.

Getting Ready to Bake
Grease trays and sprinkle with flour.
Roll out the dough to desired thickness – on to trays. Cover with cling film and let rise at room temperature for another 6 hours. For white pizzas, oil surface. For red pizzas, sprinkle with thin layer of tomato sauce.

Baking the Pizza
Bake at highest oven temperature for 20 minutes.
Check that the pizza comes easily off the pan. If it sticks, the pizza base is not ready. If it comes loose, remove from the oven.
Add your favourite toppings. Bake for another 10 minutes

CREPES WITH HERBS AND PECORINO

Serves 4-6

INGREDIENTS

300 ml of soy or vegetable milk
130 g of flour
80 ml of seed oil
1 tsp of turmeric
400 g of fresh herbs or spinach
1 garlic clove
Extra virgin olive oil
Salt and pepper to taste
12-14 thin slices of pecorino or other tasty cheese
250 g grated pecorino cheese

THE COOK

Maria Teresa Omede
Asti, Italy

Product Manager:
Le Vie del Nord

MAKING THE CREPE MIXTURE

Sift flour into a bowl. Add salt, pepper, turmeric and oil. Whisk until combined. Add soy or vegetable milk, a little at a time,slowly whisking until mixture is smooth and even. Cover with cling film and refrigeratate for an hour.

METHOD

The Sauce
Place washed fresh herbs in a pot of boiling salted water and cook for 2-3 minutes. Drain and squeeze herbs, then coarsely chop them. Heat two tbsp of oil in a pan, add whole garlic clove, chopped herbs, pinch of salt and pepper. Put on lid and cook on high for 2-4 minutes. Turn off the heat and allow to cool. Remove garlic clove. Put grated pecorino cheese into a bowl, add 20 g of extra virgin olive oil and a little salt and pepper. Add cooked herbs and mix well.

Making the crêpes
Pre-heat oven to 180° C. Grease a hot non-stick pan with a little seed oil. Ladle crêpe mixture into pan and distribute evenly. Cook for a few minutes over medium-low heat. Use spatula to turn crêpe over to cook the other side. It should be slightly golden. Remove crepe, then cook another. Stack crêpes together to keep them warm. Keep going until mixture runs out. Place a crepe on a plate. Add a thin slice of pecorino or your favourite cheese, spread with some herb sauce and then roll the crepe. Repeat, and add the rolled crepes side by side in a baking dish. Top the whole lot with more grate cheese then cook in the oven for 10-15 minutes. The cheese on top should melt and turn golden.

SEMOLINA GNOCCHI 'ROMAN STYLE'

Serves 4

INGREDIENTS

550 g of semolina
1.5 litres of fresh milk
Salt
2 sage leaves
Nutmeg
Butter
Grated Parmesan cheese

THE COOK

Roberto Chiesa
Torino, Italy

Tour Operator and GM:
Go Australia

TIPS

1) This is not classic gnocchi but a family recipe that everyone likes.
2) Sage makes them more digestible.

METHOD

The Gnocchi

Bring milk to a simmer in a saucepan with a little coarse salt, sage leaves and nutmeg. Don't let it boil. Add semolina little by little, stirring constantly with a whisk or a wooden spoon without letting it clump. Keep stirring until semolina is firm and consistent. Pour into a pan and roll it out until you get a sheet about one centimetre thick . Leave to cool. Cut cold semolina into 'gnocchi' cubes.

The Cooking

Pre-heat oven to 180° C. Grease oven dish with butter, gently add semolina and add abundant butter flakes. Place in oven and leave to cook for about 40 minutes. After 20 minutes, gently turn gnocchi and sprinkle with plenty of grated Parmesan cheese. Leave in oven until they are golden brown.

The Finale

Take out and serve hot.

BORSCHT TRADITIONAL BEETROOT SOUP

Serves 2-4

INGREDIENTS

A few rashers of bacon or speck
2 Polish or other sausages (I use kransky)
2 litres beef broth (ready-made or homemade)
4 or 5 beetroots
At least 4 other vegetables:
carrots, onions (or leeks), celery (including the leaves), potatoes, turnips, parsnips,
fresh or canned tomatoes etc.
2 large bay leaves
Sour cream
Peppercorns and salt to taste
Chopped parsley

TIPS
1) This versatile recipe depends on the vegetables you have at hand and your imagination.
2) For a vegan version, use vegetable stock.
3) For a smooth soup, remove bay leaves and sausages and blend in a blender.
4) For a richer red colour, add a tin of sliced beetroot with the juices.
5) Try adding some white wine

THE COOK

Diané Ranck
Adelaide,
South Australia

Board Director:
Connective Creativity
and keen kayaker

METHOD

Preparation
Grate or finely chop all vegetables. It's much easier to grate the root vegetables.
Wash beetroot stems and leaves to ensure there's no grit and chop these finely too. Chop the bacon.

The Cooking
Fry chopped onions and bacon (or speck) in a large pot. Add rest of vegetables and mix well.
Add stock, peppercorns, bay leaves and sausages (whole or cut into thirds) Bring to the boil and simmer until cooked.

The Finale
Serve with dollop of sour cream and chopped parsley on top.

CHESTNUT AND MUSHROOM SOUP

Serves 4-6

INGREDIENTS

Half kg of fresh mixed mushrooms
1 handful of boiled chestnuts
1 large carrot
1 onion
1 stick celery
6 cups (1.5 litres) vegetable broth
Fresh chilli
Fresh parsley
Olive oil
Salt and pepper

THE COOK

Roberto Chiesa
Torino, Italy

Tour Operator and GM:
Go Australia

TIPS

1) You can use just porcini mushrooms alone, or your favourite. A mixture of mushrooms deepens and improves the taste.
2) I often make a 'seas and mountains' version by adding fresh peeled shrimp sautéed with pepper and salt to the finished soup. Shrimp tails are also good.

METHOD

Preparation
If using dry chestnuts, soak them for at least 2 hours first. Peel and finely dice the onion, carrots and celery.

The Chestnuts and Broth
Boil the chestnuts with a bay leaf or wild fennel. When cooked, peel them well. Heat vegetable broth in a large saucepan. Remove one cup of hot broth.

The Soffritto
In a high pot (terracotta is best) prepare a classic soffritto: sauté carrots, onion and celery in plenty of olive oil and a little butter. Add mushrooms and rest of hot broth to the soffrito. Simmer for 10 minutes.

The Cooking
Meanwhile, put half the chestnuts in a blender with a cup of hot broth and mix to a thick purée. Stir purée and rest of chestnuts into the soup. Season with salt, pepper and fresh chilli to taste. Cook for another 10 minutes.

The Finale
Place slices of toasted bread or croutons in deep plates. Add soup. Serve with fresh parsley.

FRENCH ONION SOUP

Serves 2

INGREDIENTS

100 grams butter, cubed
2 kg onions
1 litre beef stock (4 cups)
4 thyme sprigs
3 parsley stalks
1 fresh bay leaf
Baguette, lightly toasted sliced diagonally
250 g grated Gruyere cheese

THE COOK

Victoria Matterson
Sydney, Australia

Fashion company founder

TIPS

1) This recipe requiresa lot of patience and attentiveness, but it's worth it.
2) Vegetarians and vegans can obviously use vegetable stock.

METHOD

Preparation

Thinly slice onions. Tie herbs together, using kitchen twine. Preheat the oven to 200° C.

The Cooking

Melt the butter in a large, heavy based saucepan over medium heat. Add onions, cover and cook until soft (about 20 minutes), stirring occasionally. Remove lid and continue to cook for one hour, or until they start to caramelise. Add stock, half a cup at a time, and simmer each time until stock has almost evaporated. Repeat until you've used 2 cups of stock. Add tied herbs to the pot. Stir in remaining 2 cups of stock and season to taste. Bring to the boil then reduce heat and simmer, scraping base of the pot to remove any caramelised bits. Simmer for around 40 minutes or until thick.

The Finale

Ladle soup into 1.5 cups capacity oven-proof bowls or ramekins and transfer to an oven tray. Scatter half cheese on top and then top each one with two slices of baguette. Add remaining cheese on top of the bread. Place in oven and cook for 5 minutes or until cheese has melted.

POTATO AND LEEK SOUP WITH CROUTONS

Serves 2

INGREDIENTS

1 cup diced leeks
1 large potato
1 litre vegetable broth/stock
Cream, crème fraîche or milk
2 slices of bread
1 garlic clove
Salt, pepper

THE COOK

Karin Marty
Zurich, Switzerland

Oceania Product Manager:
Travelhouse

TIPS

1) The more leeks or potatoes you use, the more soup you can make.
2) Add a few drops of good pumpkin seed oil before serving.

" *It's cold outside! You have one potato and half a leek left in your fridge and some slightly-stale bread in the cupboard. This warming, tasty soup with croutons can be made in no time.* "

METHOD

Preparation
Peel and dice potato. Dice leek. Crush or slice garlic.

The Cooking
In a large saucepan heat 3 cups of stock/broth, add potatoes, leek and garlic. Boil until potatoes are cooked. Transfer mixture (in stages) to a blender and blend until smooth. Return soup to the pan and add 1 cup of cream/crème fraîche/milk. Heat once more. Add pepper and salt to taste.

The Croutons
While soup is cooking, toast some thickly-sliced bread and cut it into small quares.

The Finale
Add croutons to each bowl before serving soup.

OVEN-BAKED PUMPKIN SOUP

Serves 2

INGREDIENTS

400 g Hokkaido pumpkin flesh
300 g carrots
Half an onion
2.5 cm ginger
Butter
4 cups vegetable broth
250 ml coconut milk
Salt, pepper, soy sauce
1 fresh lemon

THE COOK

Sabine Schamburger
Trier, Germany

Product Manager:
Boomerang Reisen

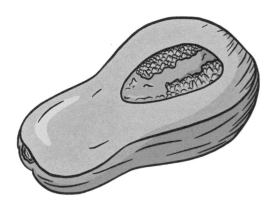

TIPS

1) These quantities serve 4 people as an entree; or 2 as a main course.
2) For a spicier soup add 1 to 2 chillies.
3) The soup can be frozen. Double the ingredients to enjoy it longer.

METHOD

Preparation
Peel and dice carrots, ginger and onions.

The Pumpkin
Cut pumpkin into large pieces and bake in the oven until tender. Even 10 minutes will make the pumpkin easier to peel and cut into smaller pieces. Alternatively, peel and dice into small pieces and bake until tender. The baking will give your soup a deep, rich flavour.

The Cooking
Sauté all vegetables – baked pumpkin, carrots, ginger and onion – in 1 tbsp of butter, in a large saucepan.
Pour in 4 cups of broth/stock. Cook for 15-20 minutes until carrots are soft.
Purée in a blender. Return to saucepan. Season with salt, pepper, soy sauce to taste and juice of half a lemon. Stir in coconut milk.

The Finale
Serve with toast or fresh bread rolls.

ROASTED CAULIFLOWER & COCONUT SOUP

Serves 6-8

INGREDIENTS

1 whole head of cauliflower
2.5 cups of vegetable stock
1 can lite coconut milk
1 yellow/brown onion
3 garlic cloves
Fresh coriander
Extra virgin olive oil
Cinnamon
Allspice
Ground coriander
Chilli flakes
2 cardamom pods
Salt, ground black pepper

THE COOK

Diana Jaquillard
Adelaide, Australia

Retired graphic designer

Foundation Board:
The Helpman Academy

TIPS

1) If you only have a small cauliflower or want to make the soup go further you can add 4 large potatoes.
(I love the texture that potatoes give to the soup.)
2) Be careful when puréeing – hot liquid can spurt and scald

METHOD

Preparation

The saucepan and baking tray are used twice. Preheat oven to 180° C. Break cauliflower into florets. Dice cauliflower leaves and onion, and peel garlic but leave whole. Divide cauliflower florets between two bowls. Mix one lot with 1 tbsp of olive oil. Toss other half with cauliflower leaves, onion and garlic, and 1 tbsp of olive oil.

The Cooking

Spread the cauliflower mix out on a baking pan. Sprinkle 1 tsp of cinnamon, a pinch of allspice, coriander and salt and black pepper to taste. Place into oven on the middle rack and cook for 25 minutes. When vegetables are done, transfer them to good-sized saucepan.
Add coconut milk and 2.5 cups of vegetable broth, 2 cardamom pods and a pinch of chilli flakes. Bring soup to a slow boil for about 5 minutes. Then simmer for another 5.
Meanwhile spread other oiled florets on the baking tray, on the top rack at 200° C and cook for 15 minutes or until golden brown.
Let soup cool a little, then add to a blender and purée until creamy.

The Finale

Pour soup into bowls, add small baked florets. Top with fresh coriander leaves, red pepper flakes and a drizzle of olive oil if desired.

CELERY WITH GORGONZOLA = FINGER FOOD

Serves 4

INGREDIENTS

12 stalks of celery
200 g of sweet Gorgonzola
100 g of mascarpone
Black pepper
12 walnut kernels

THE COOK

Maria Teresa Omede
Asti, Italy

Product Manager:
Le Vie del Nord

TIP

Adding mascaropone – or similar soft cheese – softens the overall texture and lessens the strong flavour of the gorgonzola.

METHOD

Preparation
Clean celery stalks. Cut according to whether they will be finger food (10-12 cm lengths); or used to dip (6 cm).

The Gorgonzola Dip
Put the Gorgonzola in a bowl. Mash and turn it well with a fork. Add in the mascarpone, a sprinkle of pepper, and mix until you get a smooth, fine texture.

The Finale
If you're presenting this recipe as finger food then spread cheese mixture delicately onto each long stick of celery. Leave space at one end for gripping. Arrange decoratively on a serving plate. Complete each stick with a walnut kernel. If you're offering it as a dip, place shorter celery sticks in one bowl and the gorgonzala dip in another.

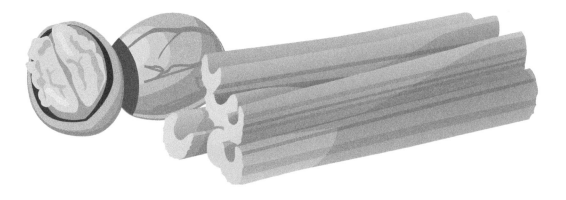

PORK AND PRAWN DUMPLINGS WITH DIPPING SAUCE

Serves 4

INGREDIENTS

1 pkt wonton wrappers (25-30 pieces)
500 g pork mince
200 g prawns
4 spring onions
1 thumb-size piece of ginger
2 garlic cloves
6 coriander sprigs
Soy sauce
Sesame oil
Sunflower oil
Black vinegar
Chilli crisp or chilli oil (optional)
Caster sugar
White pepper and sea salt

THE COOK

Rosalind Harries
Cairns, Australia

Owner:
Ros Harries Marketing

DIPPING SAUCE

Combine the following in a bowl:
1 tbsp sesame oil
60 ml soy sauce
2 tbsp black vinegar
2 tbs chilli crisp or chilli oil
1 tbsp caster sugar
Green part of the spring onion
1 tsp finely diced ginger

METHOD

Preparation
Peel and finely chop prawns. Thinly slice green and white parts of spring onion separately.
Finely dice ginger and coriander stems. Crush garlic. Put pork mince, prawns, white part
of spring onion, garlic, coriander stems, 1 tbsp of caster sugar, 1/2 tsp white pepper, 1 tsp salt
and ginger into a large bowl. Add 2 tbsp soy sauce and 1 tbsp sesame oil and mix until
everything is evenly combined.

The Dumplings
Place 1 small spoonful of the pork mixture into the centre of each wonton wrapper.
Use your finger to spread a little water along 2 edges of the wrapper. Fold the wrapper
to enclose the filling and pinch the wet side to the dry side to seal it. Try to press out all
of the air from the centre of the dumplings while sealing them.

The Cooking
Add 2 tbsp sunflower oil in large non-stick frying pan. Spread dumplings evenly and make sure
they sit flat. Over medium-high heat, cook dumplings until bases caramelise to a golden brown.
Add half a cup of water to the pan. Cover and steam dumplings for 2-3 minutes or until
cooked through.

The Finale
Garnish dumplings with fresh coriander leaves and serve with spicy dipping sauce.

PASTA
AND RICE

GRAMIGNA ALLA SALSICCI

Serves 2

INGREDIENTS

3 quality Italian sausages
1 small onion
A handful of baby spinach
(or small broccoli florets)
200 g of gramigna or similar cut of pasta
1 sprig of rosemary, finely chopped
Salt, pepper and chilli flakes to taste
Olive oil
Optional: 200 ml fresh cream or tomato paste

THE COOK

Craig Smith
A Kiwi in Italy

*Tourism Marketing
and Representation*

TIPS

1) For a creamier version add the fresh cream once sausages are almost cooked.
2) Likewise add in the tomato paste if you prefer – but not both!

METHOD

Preparation

Finely chop onions. Remove sausage meat from their casings and crumble with onion and rosemary in a mixing bowl. If you are adding small broccoli florets, boil them in some water first until almost cooked but still crunchy. If using baby spinach rip it into smaller pieces.

The Cooking

Start with a few glugs of olive oil in a large flat based pan. When hot, add your chopped onion, and sausage mix, and cook on a low heat until sausages are brown. Throw in the pre-cooked broccoli florets.

The Pasta

Boil a large pot of water, throw in a pinch of sea salt and cook pasta for two minutes less than what it says on the packet. Important! When the pasta is ready to drain, keep one glass of the cooking water aside.

The Finale

Add the almost-cooked pasta to the sausage/onion mix and add the glass of cooking water. Add the baby spinach. Turn up the heat and toss for a minute or two, or until the pasta is al dente and all is well combined. Careful not to overcook it! Plate up and add a sprinkling of grated Parmesan, a crack of pepper or some chilli flakes.

MEZZE PENNE RIGATE WITH LEEK, BACON AND PEAS

Serves 4

INGREDIENTS

Leek (green part) to taste
160 g pancetta or smoked bacon
400 g penne pasta
250 g small steamed peas
150 g Parmesan
Olive oil
Salt and pepper to taste

THE COOK

Maria Teresa Omede
Asti, Italy

Product Manager:
Le Vie del Nord

TIPS
1) Ideal for leftovers from the fridge, freezer or pantry.
2) You can use tinned, frozen or fresh peas.

METHOD

Preparation
Cut green part of leek into thin strips. Dice pancetta or smoked bacon.

The Pasta
Boil plenty of water (about 1 litre per 100 grams of pasta) in a big pot. When it boils, add salt and cook penne until it's al dente. Then drain.

The Sauce
Put 2 tbsp of oil into a large pan to heat. Add leek strips and brown for a minute.
Add diced pancetta and simmer until golden brown.
Add steamed peas and continue cooking for another 5 minutes.

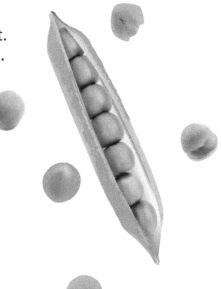

The Finale
Add penne to sauce in the pan. Add Parmesan and pepper.
Toss with a spatula or a spoon and let cook for 2 to 3 minutes.
Serve immediately.

ORECCHIETTE WITH SPINACH, SPECK AND RICOTTA

Serves 4

INGREDIENTS

350 g of dried orecchiette pasta
200 g of already boiled spinach
150 g of speck (lightly-smoked ham)
200 g of cow's milk ricotta
3 tbsp of extra virgin olive oil
1 small white onion
Salt and pepper to taste
Nutmeg (optional, but preferred)

THE COOK

Antonella Valerio
Torino, Italy

Booking: Go Asia

TIPS

1) For a creamier version add the fresh cream once sausages are almost cooked.
2) Likewise add in the tomato paste if you prefer – but not both!

METHOD

Preparation
Dice onion. Chop spinach with scissors or sharp knife.
Thickly cut speck.

The Cooking
Heat olive oil in a wok or large frypan. Add chopped onion,
when it starts to brown add diced speck. Let it cook a little, add chopped spinach,
Salt and pepper.

The Pasta
Boil orecchiette al dente in abundant salted water and drain.
Keep a cup of the cooking water aside.

The Finale
Transfer orecchiette to the pan with spinach, mix everything and add cooking water.
When water is absorbed, add ricotta. Mix everything and transfer to a serving dish.
Add sprinkling of ground nutmeg as desired.

CARNAROLI RISOTTO WITH STRAWBERRIES

Serves 2

INGREDIENTS

1.5 l light broth
1 shallot
Carnaroli rice
(2 handfuls per person plus two for the pan)
Punnet of strawberries
Sprig of mint leaves
Butter
1 cup of sparkling white wine

THE COOK

Elena Paracchi
Torino, Italy

Owner:
catviaggi.net

TIPS

1) Let the risotto rest for a few minutes with mint leaves and the mint will infuse the dish.
2) Add crumbled pistachio for a nice touch.

METHOD

Preparation
Heat broth in a saucepan. Wash and cut the strawberries into pieces. Slice shallot thinly.

Cooking the Risotto
Melt butter in a large pan. Add shallots and cook until lightly brown. Add rice to the shallot mix and stir well. Add sparkling wine to the mix and stir until it evaporates. Add broth, 1 ladle at a time, stirring constantly as you add. Let it cook for about 20 minutes, stirring regularly and while adding a few strawberries every 5 minutes. (This gives a nice pink colour.) Keep some strawberies until near the end so there are textured pieces in the final dish.

The Finale
Once rice is cooked, serve in nice bowls and decorate with mint leaves.

SICILIAN EGGPLANT ROLLS WITH SPAGHETTI

Serves 4

INGREDIENTS

2 eggplants
150 g spaghetti
400 ml tomato purée
1 garlic clove
100 g provolone cheese
40 g Parmigiano Reggiano
Several basil leaves
Extra virgin olive oil
Salt and pepper
Sunflower oil

THE COOK

Carmen Laurella
Italy

**Sales Manager
UK/Europe:**
Luxury Hotels Australia

TIPS

1) Slice the eggplant thickly, as instructed. If they break when rolling use more than one slice when making the rolls.
2) Rolls are okay in fridge to eat the next day.

" *Some days I like to go back to my origins, and this is a fabulous Sicilian dish! Basically it's spaghetti in tomato sauce rolled in fried eggplant, topped up with more sauce, basil and Pecorino cheese or Parmigiano. You will simply fall in love with this dish.* "

METHOD

Preparation
Cut eggplant into half cm slices. Sprinkle with salt and rest in a colander for 15 minutes. This helps them reduce moisture and bitterness. Dice provolone. Dice or crush garlic.

The Cooking
Spaghetti: Cook spaghetti in plenty of salted water until al dente. Drain.
Tomato sauce: Toss garlic in a little olive oil, add tomato purée and a few basil leaves. Season with salt and pepper. Cook for about 30 minutes.
Spread bottom of a baking tray with a little of the sauce. Keep some aside for topping.
Eggplant: Fry eggplant slices in plenty of sunflower oil for a couple of minutes on each side or until lightly brown. Spaghetti and sauce: add spaghetti to rest of sauce in your pan and mix well.

The Rolls
Lay cooked eggplant slices out on a bench or a board. Put a twist of saucy-spaghetti on each slice. Place two pieces of diced provolone in the centre. Roll eggplant slices into rolls.

The Finale
Place rolls onto baking tray on sauce. Cover rolls with more sauce. Sprinkle grated Parmigiano or Pecorino and more fresh basil over whole dish. Bake in a preheated oven at 190° C for 15 minutes. Serve and enjoy.

ARTICHOKE AND THYME RAVIOLI

Serves 4

INGREDIENTS

300 g flour
3 eggs
8 artichokes
160 g cow's milk ricotta
1 sprig marjoram
5 sprigs thyme
4 tbsp extra virgin olive oil
400 g Grana Padano grated
1 onion
Half cup white wine
1 garlic clove
Salt and pepper
150 g butter

TIP
If you can't find Grana Padano,
use Parmigiano Reggiano (Parmesan).

THE COOK

Sabrina Sicura
Ancona, Italy

Booking: Go Australia

MAKING THE PASTA

1) Sift flour into a bowl (keep a little aside to add later if needed).
2) Lightly beat eggs, add to flour, blend with fork.
3) Transfer mixture to a pastry board and continue kneading by hand until you create an elastic and smooth dough.
4) Wrap dough in cling film and let rest in fridge for about 30 minutes.

METHOD

The Filling
Clean, peel and chop artichokes. Finely chop onion, crush garlic. Add olive oil to a pan and sauté onions and garlic over very low heat for about 15 minutes or until onion is transparent.
Add chopped artichokes and brown them. Halfway through cooking add white wine, salt and pepper. Once cooked, blend the artichoke mixture in a food processor on a coarse setting. There should still be some larger pieces of artichoke. Transfer mixture to a bowl, add ricotta, fresh-chopped marjoram and thyme leaves, and finally grated cheese Mix everything well.

The Ravioli
At this point, you can roll the dough into a thin sheet then cut it into strips of about 10 cm width. Place the filling in centre, and close sheets on themselves. Press lightly on pastry with your finger around filling in order to let air out. Once ready, cut ravioli with a pasta bowl. Toss your artichoke ravioli parcels in flour and boil them in abundant salted water. While ravioli are cooking, melt butter in a pan and add fresh thyme.

The Finale
When ravioli are cooked, drain and sauté them in flavoured butter for a few minutes. Serve with a few leaves of thyme and a sprinkling of Grana Padano.

SCAMPI AND ZUCCHINI WITH MIXED RICE

Serves 4

INGREDIENTS

250 g Basmati rice
100 g brown Venere rice
8 scampi (4 will be used to decorate the dish)
Extra virgin olive oil to taste
2 medium zucchini (courgettes)
1 garlic clove
Salt and ground pepper to taste
Parsley and coriander to taste
Half lemon, squeezed

THE COOK

Antonella Valerio
Torino, Italy
Booking: Go Asia

TIPS

1) Scampi, prawns or shrimps can be used.
2) Use your favourite herbs.
3) This recipe is a great summer dish that can also be enjoyed at room temperature.

METHOD

The Scampi

To clean scampi, cut shell, incising entire length of the back with the help of scissors.
Cut off heads of four only. Use toothpick to remove gut tract from the back (it's a dark colour).
Careful not to break it. (The scampi with heads are used for decoration later.)
Place the scampi in a bowl with olive oil, chopped aromatic herbs, parsley, salt and pepper.
Squeeze half a lemon over scampi, making sure both sides get coated.
Cover bowl, place in fridge to marinate for two to six hours.

The Zucchini and Rice

Dice zucchini. Brown garlic clove in oil in a pan, add zucchini, season with salt and pepper and sauté.
In two separate pans, cook two different types of rice. When al dente, drain.

The Cooking

Heat a pan. Take scampi from fridge, add marinating liquid to pan. When hot, add scampi and cook for two to three minutes per side. Remove scampi, put whole ones aside.
Cut headless scampi into pieces and return to pan.

The Finale

Add sautéd zucchini and rice to scampi and mix well. Serve in bowls, each decorated with a whole scampi.

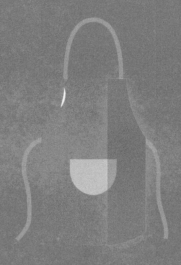

MAIN
COURSES

GRANNY PEGG'S SAUSAGE ROLLS

Serves 4-6

INGREDIENTS

400 g minced pork
600 g minced steak
4 sheets puff pastry (this makes 24 rolls)
2 eggs
Worcestershire sauce
1 onion
1 celery stick
2 garlic cloves
1 carrot
Salt and freshly ground pepper
Chilli flakes
Sesame seeds
Fenchel (fennel) seeds
Mixed herbs
Breadcrumbs

THE COOK

Rhett Lego
Munich, Germany

CEO:
Conjoint Marketing Group

METHOD

Preparation
Preheat oven to 200° C. Peel and dice onion and garlic. Grate celery and carrot.

The Sausage Mix
In a bowl, combine the two minced meats with diced garlic, onion, grated carrot, celery, 1 tbsp of Worcestershire sauce, 1 tbsp of breadcrumbs and 1 beaten egg. Add mixed herbs, chilli flakes, salt and pepper to taste. Drain any excess moisture from mixture.

The Rolls
Lay pastry sheets out on bench and cut them in half; if you start with four square sheets, you now have eight oblong ones. Share mince mixture evenly along centre of each piece of pastry. Brush one long edge with the other beaten egg. Fold pastry over to enclose the filling and press to seal it where you brushed the egg. Cut each long roll into thirds.

The Cooking
Place sausage rolls, seam down, on trays with baking paper. Brush roll tops with egg. Use a small sharp knife to pierce the tops a few times to allow steam to escape. Sprinkle with sesame seeds. Bake for 35 minutes or until golden.

The Finale
Remove from oven. Devour hot, warm or cold and with your favourite sauce.

FRANKFURTER GRÜNE SOSSE (GREEN SAUCE)

Serves 2

INGREDIENTS

10 to 12 ounces of the fresh grüne soße herbs (see right).
6 eggs
Walnut oil (or other neutral oil)
White vinegar
Greek yogurt (full cream)
Sour cream or crème fraîche
Mid-strength mustard
1 lemon
Salt, pepper, sugar
2 large potatoes, or 4 chats (enough for 2 people)

THE COOK

Susanne Stellberg
Frankfurter, Germany
and Voitsberg, Austria

**Senior Sales
and Marketing Manager:**
ULLIFINK Tourism
Marketing

Frankfurt Grüne Soße
In Frankfurt dialect, this recipe is called grie soß; and in the Frankfurt region you can buy this sauce packaged together and 'kitchen ready'.
Elsewhere you have to put it together yourselfwith fresh ingredients. The herbs, in German, are: borretsch, kerbel, kresse, petersilie, pimpinelle, sauerampfer und schnittlauch.
In English they are: borage, chervil, cress, parsley, salad burnet, sorrel and chives.

TIPS

1) Grüne Soße is traditionally served with boiled potatoes or hardboiled eggs.
2) As I prefer fried potatoes, my recipe includes them. You can also bake potatoes.
3) The green sauce also goes well with fresh asparagus or black cabbage.

METHOD

Preparation
Hardboil 6 eggs, peel and let them cool. Separate yolks from 2 of the eggs and dice them. Peel potatoes, chop into bite-size pieces and parboil. Roughly chop all the herbs, removing any thick stems.

The Grüne Soße / Green Sauce
Purée herbs in a blender, with juice of 1 lemon, 1 tsp of vinegar, and 1 tbsp of walnut oil. In a bowl, mix 125 g of yoghurt, 125 g sour cream/crème fraîche, and 1 tbsp of mustard. Stir in the blended herbs. The sauce should be mushy, by not too runny. Add two diced egg yolks. Season to taste with salt and pepper. Put sauce in the fridge for 30 minutes.

The Cooking
Meanwhile, heat 2 tbsp of olive oil in a pan, toss the potatoes until cooked to golden.

The Finale
The grüne soße is not a drizzling sauce; it's a meal. So divide the sauce between two plates and serve with two halved hardboiled eggs each and fried potatoes.

CELERY SCHNITZEL AND POTATO SALAD

Serves 2

INGREDIENTS

Celery Schnitzel
1 large celery root (celeriac)
Breadcrumbs
Sesame seeds
Parmesan cheese
1 egg
Olive oil

Potato Salad
1 kg chat (baby) potatoes
4 eggs
Fresh parsley
1 tsp caraway seeds
1 cup plain cooking or olive oil
1 egg for mayonnaise
2 onions
3 pickled gherkins
Balsamico
Salt, pepper, sugar
Dijon or seeded mustard

THE COOK

Britta Henning
Krefeld, Germany

Product Manager:
Erlebe

TIPS

1) You can use ready-made mayonnaise.
2) You can peel the potatoes before cooking.
3) The potato salad is best left to stand for a couple of hours, or overnight.
4) Use your favourite herbs.

METHOD

The Potato Salad
Cook unpeeled potatoes in salted water with 1 tsp of caraway seeds. Peel and cut into bite-size pieces and place in a large bowl. Hard boil 4 eggs. When cool, cut in half.

The Mayonnaise
Dice onions and gherkins. In a blender mix 1 egg, 2 tsps of Balsamico, 1 tsp of mustard, pinch of salt, pepper and sugar. While blending, slowly add 1 cup of oil. Add gherkin and onion. Mix into the cooked potatoes. Add the hard-boiled eggs. Put in the fridge.

The Schnitzels
Wash and peel celery root. Slice into pieces 2 cm thick. Cook slices in salted water for 6 minutes. Remove, dry on paper towel. In a large bowl, beat one egg, a dash of milk and season with salt and pepper. Mix 2 cups of breadcrumbs, with 1 tbsp sesame seeds, 2 tbsp Parmesan cheese and any favourite spices. Spread evenly on a large flat plate or chopping board. Dip celery root slices in egg mix, coating all sides. Do the same in the breadcrumb mix. You can repeat these two steps to get a deeper crumbing. Heat some olive oil in a fry pan and cook the schnitzels for about 4 minutes on each side. When they look nice and crusty, remove from the pan.

The Finale
Serve the schnitzels with the potato salad.

FRIED ARTICHOKES

Serves 2

INGREDIENTS

2 artichokes
Plain flour
Extra virgin olive oil
Salt

TIPS

1) Use kitchen gloves to avoid blackening your fingers.
2) Double the number of artichokes to feed more people.

THE COOK

Marina Fidele
Milan, Italy
Travel Agent:
Mondo for You

METHOD

Preparation
Fill a large bowl with fresh water and juice of half a lemon. Remove hardest outer leaves from artichokes and trim tips off. Cut artichoke into 4 slices and remove internal 'beard'.
Cut each slice in half lengthways. Put eight slices in lemon water to soak until you're ready to fry. Cover a large dish with absorbent paper.

The Cooking
Put half cup of white flour in mixing bowl or plate. Toss artichoke slices in and lightly coat them in flour. Heat 2 tbsp of olive oil in a non-stick pan. Fry slices of artichoke slices.
Very important: Oil should be very hot; fry no more then 5-6 pieces at a time for 3-5 minutes each.

The Finale
Transfer to absorbent paper for a few minutes. Season with salt – this is essential.
Serve hot.

BAHIAN SEAFOOD MOQUECA

Serves 2

INGREDIENTS

White fish: 150 g per person
200 ml coconut milk
1 large onion
1 yellow capsicum
1 red capsicum
Cummin
Fresh coriander
1 lime
Olive oil
Salt and pepper

THE COOKS

**Claudio Del Bianco
Owner:**
Del Bianco Travel

in collaboration with
Chef Simone Almeida
Rio/Brasil

Chef:
cookinrio.com

TIP
You can add shrimps to the recipe for a different flavour.

METHOD

Preparation
Cut fish into 2 cm slices. Slice onion and capsicums into rings. Mix juice of one lemon with 1 tsp of cummin, and salt and black pepper to taste. Marinate fish for 10 minutes in lime juice mixture.

The Cooking
Heat 1 tbsp of oil in a large pan, and stir in capsicums and onion. Add marinated fish, pour in coconut milk. Cook everything on medium heat for 25 minutes or until the capsicums soften.

The Finale
Serve in bowls and garnish with coriander.

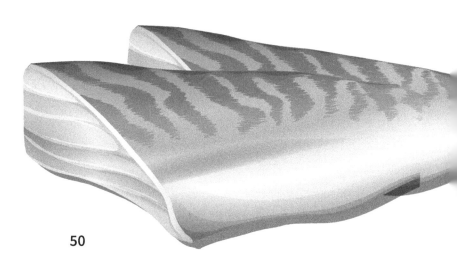

CHINESE STEAMED FISH WITH GINGER AND SHIITAKE

Serves 1-2

INGREDIENTS

1 kg fresh, whole Barramundi
or other whole fish
5 cm piece of fresh ginger
1 garlic clove
4 shiitake mushrooms
1 stalk spring onions
Light soy sauce
Shaoxing wine or rice wine
Seame oil
Freshly ground white pepper

THE COOK

Swee Wah Yew
Adelaide, Australia

Artist

TIPS

1) Set up the steamer first. You need a tiered metal steamer – or a wok/deep skillet/pot – as long as it has a lid. In the bottom of the wok place a round metal trivet for the fish plate to sit on. Fill the pot with enough water to just cover the trivet.
2) I use barramundi but you can use many kinds of whole fish like sea bass, snapper, cod, grouper.

" *For Chinese, a fish served whole is a symbol of prosperity especially on the Chinese New Year. Fish has ongoing significance because the Chinese word for fish – yu – sounds like nian nian you yu which means (may you have) abundance year after year,an increase in prosperity. It is believed eating a whole fish will help your wishes come true in the year to come.* "

METHOD

Preparation
Clean fish (remove scales, guts, gills, etc.) and pat dry. Soak shiitake in warm water then slice thinly. Peel and dice ginger. Crush garlic clove. Cut spring onion into 5 cm lengths.

The Sauce
Combine 4 tbsp light soy sauce, 2 tbsp shaoxing wine/rice wine, .25 tsp sesame oil in a bowl.

The Cooking
Lay the whole fish on a plate and spoon sauce over it. Scatter half of ginger strips and shiitake mushrooms over the fish. Heat water in your wok/skillet (see Tips). As soon as water is boiling, place your fish on its plate onto the trivet and fit lid. Reduce to a simmer and steam fish for 5-8 minutes. While waiting, fry the rest of ginger and garlic with ground white pepper in olive oil.

The Finale
As soon as fish is done steaming, remove from the wok. Sprinkle fish with spring onions and fried ginger and garlic. Serve with steamed jasmine rice.

GINGER AND CHILLI BAKED FISH

Serves 1

INGREDIENTS

175 g Murray cod or other thick white fish fillet, like snapper or barramundi (preferably skinless)
1 garlic clove
15 g fresh ginger
1 spring onion
1 red birds eye chilli or chilli flakes to taste
1 small lime
Fresh coriander
Olive or canola oil

TIPS
1) Serve with your favourite vegetables.
2) I often have with potatoes, fresh asparagus and corn on the cob.

THE COOK

Heidi Newport
Sydney Australia

Consultant:
Global Village Travel

METHOD

Preparation

Preheat oven to 200° C. Peel and thinly slice garlic and red chilli. Peel ginger and cut into matchsticks. Trim and diagonally slice spring onion. Cut lime in half.

The Cooking

Place a rectangle of kitchen foil, or baking paper, on a baking tray and drizzle with oil. Place fish (skin-side down) on one half of the foil, leaving enough foil to cover. Sprinkle fish with garlic, ginger, spring onion, chilli and squeezed juice of half the lime. Season with sea salt and plenty of ground black pepper. Fold foil over fish to cover and roll edges to seal fish inside. Don't make the parcel too tight as space is needed to create steam to cook the fish.

Bake in the oven for 12-15 minutes, or until fish is cooked and flakes into large pieces when prodded with a fork.

The Finale

Carefully open foil parcel and lift or slide fish on to a warmed plate.
Spoon cooking juices over fish, top with coriander and it's done!
Serve with lime wedges and vegetables of your choice.

GRAVLAX-STYLE SALMON

Serves 1-2

INGREDIENTS

250 g salmon (no skin, no bones)
Coarse salt
Caster sugar
Pink pepper
Coriander seeds
1 lemon
1 bunch of dill
Olive oil
Sherry vinegar
Salt and ground pepper
1 fennel bulb
1 clementine (or tangerine)

THE COOK

Aurelia Devilliers-Fezay
Villemomble, France
Product Manager:
Australie Tours

TIPS

1) As I don't like dill I use fresh coriander.
2) The longer you leave the salmon in the fridge to marinate, the deeper the flavour.
3) This salmon dish is ideal with a simple salad of cherry tomatoes, avocado and romane lettuce.
4) If you can't get a clementine then a tangerine or mandarin will do.

METHOD

The Preparation
Wash and dry fresh dill (or coriander) and dice roughly. Grate lemon zest. Crush 1 tsp of coriander seeds. Finely chop fennel.

The Salmon Marinade
In a salad bowl, mix 250 g of coarse salt with 80 g of caster sugar. Mix in lemon zest, crushed coriander seeds, 1 tsp of pink pepper, and half diced dill. Place piece of salmon on sheet of cling film and coat with mixture. Form a roll with cling film around piece of salmon and place in fridge for at least 20 minutes to marinate. When done remove cling film, run salmon under a trickle of cold water, then place it on absorbent paper. Leave in a cool place to dry.

The Herb Dressing
In a blender, mix the rest of diced dill and 6 tbsp of olive oil into a smooth mixture. Pour into a bowl, stir in 2 tbsp of sherry vinegar, and season with salt and pepper.

The Finale
Cut marinated salmon into 1 cm slices. (You can present on a serving dish or serve on separate plates.) Spread herb dressing on salmon. Peel and divide clementine into pieces. Add fennel, clementine pieces and a few sprigs of dill harmoniously to the plates.

SALMON, FETA AND VEGETABLE BAKE

Serves 4

INGREDIENTS

4 x 200 g skinless salmon fillets
4 zucchinis
250 g cherry tomatoes
150 g Feta crumbled
2 medium-size red onions
2 baby fennel
2 small lemons
Olive oil
Dried oregano
Fresh basil

TIPS

1) The best thing about this dish, apart from the fresh, clean flavours, is that you only use one pan!
2) This dish is great with a green salad or buttered baby spinach.

THE COOK

Julie Weber
Benahavis, Spain

Director:
MTD Australia

METHOD

Preparation

Preheat oven to 200° C or 180° C fan forced.
Cut zucchini in half lengthways then in half crossways. Quarter onions and cut fennel into 1 cm thick slices. Thinly slice lemons. Line a large baking tray with baking paper.

The Cooking

Arrange zucchini, onion and fennel on prepared tray. Drizzle with 1 tbsp of oil, sprinkle with 1 tsp of oregano, and season with salt and pepper. Roast vegetables for 20 minutes or until tender and golden. Place salmon in with vegetables and top with lemon slices.
Add tomatoes and crumble feta over the top. Roast for another 15 minutes or until salmon flakes easily when tested with a fork.

The Finale

Serve onto plates, garnish with fresh basil leaves, a squeeze of lemon juice and drizzle of olive oil.

STUFFED CUTTLEFISH

Serves 4

INGREDIENTS

4 large cuttlefish (at least 200 g each)
1 onion
3 small carrots
6 tbsp of extra virgin olive oil
2 eggs
400 g of tinned peeled tomatoes
1 sachet of saffron
Breadcrumbs to taste
Fine salt and freshly ground pepper
1 sprig of parsley or coriander

THE COOK

Antonella Valerio
Torino, Italy
Booking: Go Asia

TIPS

1) The filling must fill half of the cuttlefish bag, since, like all cephalopods, they tend to shrink when cooked, so if the filling is too full it will tend to come out or break the cuttlefish bag.
2) Dissolve the saffron in 1 tbsp of water before adding to the sauce

METHOD

Preparation
Hard boil one of the eggs, then peel and let it cool. Peel and finely chop onion and carrots.

The Filling
Fry half the onion in olive oil, add half the carrots and cook for a few minutes. Add chopped cuttlefish fins and tentacles and cook for a few minutes more. Remove from heat and put filling in a large bowl to cool. Crumble the yolk and dice the white of one boiled egg into a bowl.
Beat second egg, add salt, pepper, parsley or coriander and mix into cooked egg.
Add breadcrumbs, as required; the filling should be firm but not hard. Half fill the cuttlefish bag with the filling and close with one or two toothpicks.

The Sauce and the Cooking
Fry remaining carrot and onion in a large pan until tender. Add tomatoes and saffron, cook for 10 minutes. Add stuffed cuttlefish and cover with a lid. Continue cooking on low for 30 minutes. Turn cuttlefish every now and then to prevent them from sticking to the bottom.

The Finale
When cuttlefish are cooked, arrange them on a serving plate, whole or cut into slices, if large and add tomato sauce.

CHICKEN STIR FRY IN NEVER-FAIL SAUCE

Serves 4

INGREDIENTS

300 g chicken breast fillet
2 garlic cloves
1 red birds eye chilli
Fresh ginger
Yellow capsicum
1 brown onion
Fresh coriander
Olive oil
Vegetables: asparagus, snow peas and cabbage
Honey, the runny kind
Soy sauce (salt-reduced)
Chinese cooking wine
Oyster sauce
Noodles or rice

THE COOK

Heidi Newport
Sydney Australia

Consultant:
Global Village Travel

TIPS

1) I always grate a lot of ginger and store in a container in the fridge. A little water helps it keep longer.
2) You can of course use whatever veggies you like in this dish.

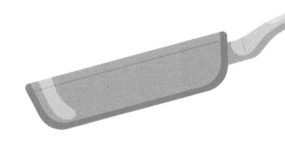

METHOD

Preparation
Cut chicken breast into small wedges. Peel and thinly slice chilli (without seeds) and garlic. Dice capsicum and onions. Grate a tbsp of ginger. Prepare/dice cabbage, asparagus, snow peas and any other veggies you are using.

The Sauce
Mix 2 tbsp honey, 2 tbsp soy sauce, 1 tbsp oyster sauce and 2 tbsp Chinese cooking wine in a bowl.

The Cooking
Heat a tbsp of oil in a wok. Stir fry chicken pieces, then set aside. Add a little more oil to the wok then toss garlic, ginger and chilli for about 30 seconds, add capsicum and onion for a couple of minutes, then the rest of vegetables and stir fry to your preferred tenderness.
Return chicken to the pan and stir. Add sauce and stir in for about minute so it warms up.

The Finale
Serve with noodles or steamed rice and garnish with coriander.

CHICKEN TAJINE WITH DRIED APRICOTS AND PRUNES

Serves 4-6

INGREDIENTS

100 g dried apricots
100 g prunes
550 ml of dry apple cider (hard or soft)
1 kg of boneless skinless chicken thighs
2 onions
1 garlic clove
3 carrots
1 tbsp curry powder
50 g flour
150 ml chicken stock
Juice of two oranges
Olive oil
1 tbsp of brown sugar
Salt and pepper
Rice or cous cous

THE COOK

Nicolo Dalponte
Washington DC, USA
Consultant:
World Bank

TIPS
1) It's great served on rice with saffron or in coconut milk.
2) Or serve on cous cous.
3) A side dish of your choice of chutney is a great addition. I recommend mango-coconut or mint.

METHOD

Preparation
Soak apricots and prunes in cider for at least 1 hour or, even better, overnight. Peel and dice onions, garlic and carrots.

The Cooking
Heat 2 tbsp of oil in a pan and fry outside of chicken thighs for a minute or two then put them in a casserole dish with diced carrots.
Fry onions until they are lightly browned. Sprinkle 1 tbsp of curry powder and 50 g of flour into pan and stir. Add stock and apricots and prunes with ider and bring to boil and let thicken. Stir in orange juice, garlic and sugar and season to taste.
Pour mixture over chicken thighs in the casserole dish and cook in oven for 2 hours at 170° C.

The Finale
Serve over couscous or rice.

DUCK BREAST FILLETS WITH CUMQUATS

Serves 6

INGREDIENTS

12 boneless duck breasts, skin on
500 g cumquats, preferably sweet-skinned variety
Sugar
Brandy
2-4 small hot chillis
Fresh coriander
Ground chilli powder
Salt and ground black pepper

TIP

This dish goes brilliantly with fresh green beans or minted peas; and parsnip mashed with roasted red onion, cumin, fresh grated ginger, fresh coriander and sour cream.

THE COOK

Diana Jaquillard
Adelaide, Australia

Retired graphic designer

Foundation Board:
The Helpman Academy

METHOD

Preparation
Chop 4 tbsp of coriander. Finely dice chilli. Prick duck skins. Preheat oven to 200° C.

Glazing the Cumquats
In a large pan, bring 2 cups of water, half a cup of brandy, and 1 cup of sugar to the boil. Slice one third of cumquats in half, and prick the rest a few times. Add them all to brandy, mix and simmer for 60–90 minutes, or until liquid is syrupy.

The Duck Breasts
Place duck breasts skin side up on an oiled baking dish. Season with salt and pepper. Sprinkle with fresh chillis, coriander and a little chilli powder. Spoon half cumquat syrup over breasts and place a few sliced cumquats on each.

The Cooking
Bake breasts for 30-40 minutes, or until done to your liking. Check regularly if you like them pink and baste with more syrup at least once. When cooked, drain duck fat from pan.

The Finale
Serve duck breasts on heated plates. Spoon meaty syrup juices over duck, then add more cumquats. Garnish elegantly with a few stems of fresh coriander. Serve with your favourite vegetable or see tips.

MILANESE-STYLE OSSIBUCHI

Serves 4

INGREDIENTS

1.2 kg veal ossibuchi (4 pieces of 300 g)
4 cups meat broth/stock
1 golden onion
50 g of flour
White wine
Extra virgin olive oil
Butter
Salt and black pepper
1 sprig parsley
2 cloves garlic
Zest of 1 lemon

THE COOK

Roberto Chiesa
Torino, Italy

Tour Operator and GM:
Go Australia

TIPS

1) The sauce needs to thicken, but if it thickens too much, add a little more stock.
2) I often add a add a little tomato to the sauce to bind the ingredients.
3) The ossibuchi are usually served with risotto alla milanese (risotto with saffron) but you can also serve them with peas or polenta.

METHOD

Preparation
Peel and dice onions. Season 50 g of flour with salt and pepper and coat the ossobuchi.

The Cooking
Add 1 tbsp of oil to large pan that you'll be cooking everything in and cook onions on low heat for 5 minutes. Add 1 cup white wine and cook onions until golden, then remove from pan and set aside. Add 40 g of butter and 1 tbsp of oil to onion pan and reheat. Place ossobuchi in pan and brown over medium-high heat for 4 minutes. Then gently turn them and sauté for another 2 minutes until a crust is formed over the meat. Add another cup of wine and simmer the ossobuchi until the wine evaporates. Pour stock over ossobuchi to almost cover it. Add cooked onions. Cover pan with a lid and cook ossobuchi and sauce over low heat for 35 minutes. Gently turn ossobuchi and continue cooking for another 25 minutes.

The Gremolada
While ossobuchi are cooking prepare the special condiment. Dice garlic, chop parsley, grate lemon zest and mix the three together.

The Finale
When ossobuchi are cooked, dress the meat with gremolada and cover pan again for a couple of minutes. Serve on warm plates with your choice of side dish. See my Tips.

PENANG CHAR KOAY TEOW (FLAT RICE NOODLE)

Serves 4

INGREDIENTS

8-12 large shrimps/prawns
2 Chinese sausage
10-12 blood cockles
1 packet of flat rice noodles
4 garlic cloves
Preserved radish
Bean sprouts
1 bunch Chinese chives
Cooking oil or pork lard
Chilli paste
4 eggs
Soy sauce and black soy sauce
Oyster sauce

THE COOK

Swee Wah Yew
Adelaide, Australia

Artist

TIPS

1) Blood cockles are a must for some people but are optional.
2) Use dice fish cakes instead or as well.
3) Use freshly-made noodles if possible.
4) If you use dried noodles soak in hot water.
5) Use pork lard if you can. It is the secret to the rich silky taste.
6) The 'chai poh' – preserved radish – adds the umami flavour to the dish.

METHOD

Preparation
Peel and dice garlic. Chop 1 tbsp of radish. Cut chives into 4 cm lengths. Slice Chinese sausage. Peel shrimps/prawns and remove the gut. Extract blood cockles from their shells.

The Cooking
Heat wok with 3 tbsp of cooking oil or pork lard. Toss in garlic and 1 tbsp of preserved radish, then add prawns, fish cakes, Chinese sausage, chilli paste (to taste) and continue to stir frying until prawns are nearly done. Add rice noodles, tossing vigorously to prevent them sticking to the wok. Once they're mixed, add 4 tbsp soy sauce, 1.5 tbsp black soy sauce and 3 tbsp oyster sauce. Add large handful of bean sprouts and toss for 10 seconds. Push all ingredients to one side of wok and put 1 tbsp of oil to the empty space. Break eggs into hot oil, then cover with rice noodle mix. Cook eggs, covered in this way, for about 20 seconds. Add chives, blood cockles and stir well.

The Finale
Serve hot.

PORK FILLET WITH WARM BOK CHOY SALAD

Serves 4

INGREDIENTS

2 pork fillets (250 g each)
3 red radishes
1 tbsp pickled ginger
1 bunch of coriander
1 spring onion
2 birdseye chillies
6 bok choy
Coriander seeds
Honey
Soy sauce
Olive oil
Sesame oil

THE COOK

Judith North
Gold Coast, Australia

UK/Europe Sales:
Baillie Lodges

TIPS

1) You can use other green vegetables like cabbage or spinach instead of bok choy or in addition to it.

METHOD

Preparation

In a bowl mix 50 ml honey, 100 ml soy sauce, 50 ml olive oil and 1 tsp sesame oil.
Pour three-quarters of mixture over pork fillets and marinate for half an hour.
Julienne radishes, pluck coriander leaves, thinly slice spring onion and chillies, separate bok choy leaves, and crush 2 tsps of coriander seeds. Preheat oven to 220° C.

The Cooking

Remove pork from marinade and discard liquid. Brown meat on all sides in a hot pan, then transfer to oven tray and bake for 15 minutes. Remove, cover tray with foil and rest for 10 minutes. Meanwhile, mix radish, pickled ginger and fresh coriander in a bowl. Heat 1 tbsp of olive oil in wok or pan, until smoking, then add spring onion, chilli and bok choy. Toss over high heat until bok choy is just wilted. Add radish mix to the wok, pour over most of reserved marinade and toss well. Remove from heat.

The Finale

To serve, divide salad among 4 serving plates and sprinkle with crushed coriander seeds.
Cut pork fillets into thick slices and place next to (or on) warm salad.
Drizzle with remaining marinade.

RETRO BURGER

Serves 1

INGREDIENTS

100 g mince beef
Round bread roll
Sliced onion
Sliced tomato
Tin of beetroot
Cheese slice
Iceberg lettuce
BBQ Sauce

Optional:
Bacon rasher
1 Egg
Pineapple ring

TIPS
1) Double or triple the ingredients if you need to feed more than just yourself.
2) You can use tomato sauce (ketchup) rather than BBQ sauce.

THE COOK

Paul Cooper
Phillip Island,
Australia

Marketing Manager:
Sydney Melbourne
Touring

METHOD

Preparation
Peel, half and slice onion, slice tomato, chop lettuce, and cut bread roll in half. Roll minced beef into a 100 g ball.

The Cooking
Cook mince by flattening ball into a patty shape on a pre-heated hotplate, turning to cook both sides. Season with salt and pepper to taste. Add onion to the hotplate to caramelise it. Toast inside of buns on a grill. For optional and delicious taste and flavour, fry bacon rasher, egg and/or pineapple ring on the hotplate while cooking minced beef. When rolls are lightly toasted, butter them. On the bottom half add slices of cheese, tomato and beetroot and some lettuce. When mince patty is cooked, scoop onion on top of it, remove from hot plate and carefully put both on top of salad. Add some BBQ sauce.
If you're adding egg, bacon and/or pineapple place on top of everything.

The Finale
Place top half of the toasted bread roll on this pile of deliciousness and enjoy.

PORK AND GINGER MEATBALLS WITH CHAO RUBING HALOUMI

Serves 4

INGREDIENTS

The Meatballs
500 g minced pork
30 g self-raising flour
2.5 tbsp soy sauce
1 tbsp hoisin sauce
Fresh ginger
2 garlic cloves
1 small red chilli

For the Chao rubing Fried haloumi
400 g haloumi
1 onion
1 garlic clove
Green or red capsicum
Fresh ginger
5 dried long red chillis
Sichuan peppercorns
4 spring onions
Vegetable oil
Light soy sauce
Chinkiang vinegar
Sichuan pepper oil
10 cherry tomatoes

THE COOK

Susanne Larsson
Oslo, Norway

Travel Designer:
Blixen Tours

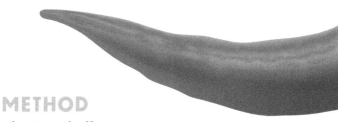

METHOD

The Meatballs
Dice garlic and chillis, grate 2 tbsp of ginger. Use hands to mix these with 2.5 tbsp soy sauce, 1 tbsp hoisin sauce, 30 g flour and pork mince in a large bowl. Wash then lightly oil your hands with vegetable oil. Roll pork mixture into walnut-sized balls. Place balls on baking tray lined with foil, flattening them slightly and roast them in the oven at 240C for 15 minutes, turning occasionally, until browned and cooked through.

The Chao rubing and Fried Halloumi
Preparation: Slice the haloumi (to share with four people). Cut the onion into wedges, dice 1 garlic clove and 5 red chillis (remove seeds), dice a quarter of the capsicum and grate 1 tbsp of ginger. Dice the spring onion, keep some green tops aside for garnish.
The Cooking: Heat 4 tbsp of oil in a wok. Add haloumi, turning until golden. Remove cheese with a slotted spoon, set aside on absorbent paper and discard oil. Heat 1.5 tbsp of fresh oil, and stir fry onion and garlic for 3 minutes. Add capsicum, ginger, chilli, 1 tbsp Sichuan peppercorns and spring onion and stir-fry for 30 seconds. Return haloumi to the wok. Add 1 tbsp soy sauce, 1 tsp vinegar and 2 tsp Sichuan pepper oil. Stir-fry for two minutes. If mixture is dry, add a splash of water.

The Finale
Add cherry tomatoes to warm through. Serve hot and garnish with spring onions.

TRADITIONAL LIÈGE BALLS

Serves 6+

INGREDIENTS

300 g of minced beef
700 g of minced pork
4 slices of white bread
5 onions
1 bunch of parsley
2 eggs
Salt, pepper and nutmeg
Breadcrumbs
4 cloves
2 bay leaves
Liège syrup (or similar)
Currants
Red wine vinegar
1 litre of meat stock (broth)
Thyme
Brown sugar
A few juniper berries

THE COOK

Marc A. Lambert
Bruxelles, Belgique
Consultant:
Qvo Vadis Tourism

METHOD

Preparation
Peel and dice onion. Chop parsley and beat two eggs. Soak bread in milk.

The Meatballs
In a large bowl mix mince, bread, onion, parsley and egg. Knead with your hands, adding breadcrumbs a little at a time to get a firm mixture. Season with salt, pepper and nutmeg to taste, then shape into balls of about 120 grams (golf ball size). Heat some butter in a heavy-based saucepan or cook pot, and fry the meatballs until brown. They don't need to be cooked through. Remove from their juice and set aside.

The Sauce
Use the meatballs' cooking juice to brown the onions and a pinch of thyme. Stir in 4 tbsp of brown sugar to form a caramel. Deglaze with a drizzle of red wine vinegar. Add 1 litre of meat stock (or a litre of water and 2 stock cubes). Bring to the boil. Add 2 tbsp of real Liège syrup, 4 cloves, 2 bay leaves and a few juniper berries. Return meatballs to the sauce, place a lid on the pot and cook for 30 to 35 minutes. In the last five minutes stir in 2 tbsp of currants. If you prefer a thicker sauce add a little cornstarch.

The Finale
Serve with fries and salad, or mashed potato.

TIPS
1) Liège syrup (syrop de Liège) is a jelly-like jam of apples and pears. It comes from the Liège region of Belgium.
2) You can substitute corn syrup or molasses for Liège syrup
3) Liège meatballs are ideal with fries and salad; or creamy mashed potato.

VENISON GOULASH

Serves 4

INGREDIENTS

1 kg venison (deer) goulash
2 onions
1 carrot
1 stick of celery
300 ml red wine (good one!)
400 ml venison (meat) stock
Red wine vinegar or balsamico
Red currant jam or Lingon berry jam
Tomato paste
Venison spice mix
Salt and pepper
Thyme
6 juniper berries
Salt and pepper
3 bay leaves
3 cloves
Olive oil

THE COOK

Conny Schütz
Munich, Germany

Market Manager Germany:
Tourism Fiji

TIPS

1) The original recipe features lingon berries, but I use my dad's homemade red currant jam.
2) I also add a touch of mustard to the sauce in the end.

METHOD

Preparation
Dice onions, carrot and celery. Drain goulash, cut into bite-sized pieces and pat dry.

The Cooking
Heat 2 tbsp of oil in a roaster or large saucepan. Brown pieces of goulash then set aside.
In the meaty sauce of the pan, fry the onions, carrots and celery, stir in 1 tbsp of tomato paste and gradually deglaze with half red wine and venison stock. Return meat to the pan, season with salt and pepper, then add remaining wine, stock, venison spice mix, thyme, cloves and bay leaves. Stir in 2 tbsp of red wine vinegar, and 2 tbsp of the red current jam. Cover with a lid and simmer for about two to three hours until the meat is tender. Stir occasionally. Remove the lid for the last half of an hour so that the sauce can thicken better. Add 2 tbsp jam, juniper berries (squash them a little) and salt and pepper to taste. If the sauce is too thin, add a bit of cornstarch (dissolved in a little water first).

The Finale
Serve with vegetables of your choice. It's best with red cabbage, with a bit of apple cooked into it, or with potatoes of some kind – dumplings or mashed.

CABBAGE PAN WITH MINCED MEAT

Serves 2

INGREDIENTS

300 g ground beef (or diced chicken)
1 stick of celery
2 carrots
1 leek
Half a pointed cabbage
(hispi or sweetheart cabbage)
Chilli
Other vegetables:
cauliflower, beans, broccoli, brussel sprouts, snow peas
Salt, pepper, cumin
1-2 tbsp of tomato paste
1 tbsp vegetable broth powder
Olive oil

THE COOK

Sabine Schamburger
Trier, Germany

Product Manager:
Boomerang Reisen

TIPS

1) This is a great for leftover vegetables, so the quantities don't really matter.
2) Vegetarians can leave out the meat.
3) The only important thing is the order in which the vegetables are cooked, to ensure they're ready at the same time and not overcooked.
4) You can season it differently too, with Asian-style flavours of soy sauce, cilantro/coriander and ginger.

METHOD

Preparation
Finely dice celery and chilli, cut leek into rings, dice cabbage in strips, (remove stalk).
Peel and grate carrots, dice any other vegetables into small bite size pieces: the brussels sprouts in half, the broccoli and/or cauliflower into small florets.

The Cooking
Fry the ground beef in a pan with olive oil until well separated. Season with salt, pepper and cumin. Add celery, chilli, carrots and leek to pan and sauté.
Add cauliflower next then, after a few minutes, the Brussels sprouts and broccoli.
Stir in 2 tbsp of tomato paste to give it a more roasted flavour. When all vegetables are almost cooked (but still firm to the bite), add pointed cabbage. Add vegetable broth powder on top of pointed cabbage and deglaze with half a glass of water and then cover pan with a lid. Simmer (or rather, steam) over a low heat for about 5 minutes until liquid is pretty much absorbed.

The Finale
Add sour cream before serving. Or serve on separate plates with dollops of sour cream.

SAUSAGES INFUSED WITH TOMATO SAUCE

Serves 4-6

INGREDIENTS

1 kg of pork sausage
1 l of dry white wine
1 sprig of rosemary
3 juniper berries
Black peppercorns
Chilli powder
2 bay leaves
Salt
750 g (3 tins) of tomatoes (or purée)
Parmesan cheese

TIPS

1) Pork sausages dressed with tomato sauce go perfectly with polenta; or with fugassin (see my recipe for fugassin elsewhere).

THE COOK

Roberto Chiesa
Torino, Italy
Tour Operator and GM:
Go Australia

METHOD

Preparation
Cut sausage into 5 cm lengths. Put in a bowl, add 3 juniper berries, a sprig of rosemary and 3 black peppercorns. Cover with white wine and leave to infuse for about 4 hours. If you're not using tomato purée, pass tomatoes through a sieve.

The Cooking
Drain sausages and brown them over high heat in a high pot until they are golden brown. Pour tomatoes over sausages. Add a little water, bay leaves, a small pinch of chilli powder and salt to taste. Cook over low heat for about 3 hours.

The Finale
Serve with polenta, fuggasin, or your favourite bread. Sprinkle with fresh Parmesan.

OTTOLENGHI SWISS CHARD AND RICOTTA PIE

Serves 4

INGREDIENTS

500 g swiss chard (silverbeet)
1 medium onion
3 garlic cloves
2 eggs
50 g Parmesan
150 g dolcelatte (a mild blue cheese)
4 spring onions
1 rectangular sheet puff pastry
100 g ricotta
Nigella seeds
Unsalted butter
Olive oil

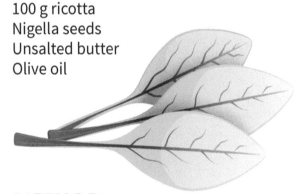

THE COOK

Susanne Stellberg
Frankfurt, Germany
and Voitsberg, Austria

Senior Sales and Marketing Manager:
ULLIFINK Tourism
Marketing

TIPS

1) If you can't get chard you can use spinach and green asparagus.
2) Nigella seeds are an ancient seed, also known as black cumin, kalonji, fennel flower, Roman coriander and blackseed.

METHOD

Preparation

Peel and slice onion. Crush garlic. Trim and slice spring onions. Beat one whole egg and, separately, the yolk of another. Preheat oven to 200° C (180C fan). Separate chard leaves and stems, cut stems to 1 cm lengths and shred the leaves.

The Chard Filling

Heat 25 g of butter and a tbsp of oil in a large pan, fry the onion until well browned. Add chard stems, cook until softened. Stir in chard leaves, garlic, salt and black pepper to taste. Cook for 4 minutes, until leaves wilt and release some of their liquid. Turn off heat, leave to cool for 20 minutes, then stir in whole beaten egg, grated Parmesan, crumbled dolcelatte and spring onions.

The Pie and the Cooking

Line base and sides of a rectangular baking tin with greaseproof paper. Drape puff pastry over it, ensuring it fits well, covers the bottom of the tin and extends up over the sides. Spoon chard mixture onto pastry, spreading it evenly to cover base. Top with a few tbsp of ricotta. Sprinkle 2 tbsp of nigella seeds on top. Fold top edges of pastry so it's thicker. Brush edge with beaten egg yolk. Bake for 40 minutes, or until golden and pastry is cooked through.

The Finale

Leave to cool for about 15 minutes before serving.

BROCCOLI PATTIES WITH PARMESAN & GOATS CHEESE

Serves 4

INGREDIENTS

For 8 muffins:
300 g broccoli
1 garlic clove
2 eggs
60 g flour
Sweet chilli powder
Salt and pepper
40 g Parmesan
110 g goat cheese log

THE COOK

Aurelia Devilliers-Fezay
Villemomble, France

Product Manager:
Australie Tours

TIP
Serve your patties without the goat cheese topping or with your favourite cheese instead.

METHOD

Preparation
Crush garlic. Grate 40 g of Parmesan. Slice goat cheese into 8 pieces. Preheat oven to 200° C. Finely chop, grate or vitamise the broccoli.

The Cooking
In a bowl, beat 2 eggs & mix in garlic, 60 g of flour, salt, pepper & chilli powder to taste. Transfer to saucepan, add Parmesan & stir in broccoli. Stir over a low heat for 5-6 minutes. Pour mixture into a buttered or oiled muffin tin. Add a slice of goat cheese on top of each muffin. Bake in oven for 25-30 minutes.

The Finale
Serve alone as a snack, or with salad.

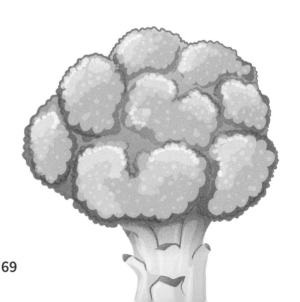

CAVOLO NERO QUICHE WITH PURPLE CAULIFLOWER

Serves 4

INGREDIENTS

Crust
Cold butter
Flour
Cold milk

Filling
Your favourite cheese to grate
1 bunch Cavolo nero
1 onion
1 purple cauliflower
Pitted olives
3 eggs
Milk
Salt, pepper, nutmeg and fresh herbs
(oregano, thyme, basil) to taste

THE COOK

Mary Retzler
Rome, Italy

**Marketing
and PR Coordinator:**
Cathay Pacific

TIPS
1) Cavolo nero is a type of kale, also known as Tuscan kale or black cabbage.
2) If you lack time or energy, use pre-made pastry sheets.

METHOD

The Preparation
Dice onions, chop cavolo nero into small pieces, separate cauliflower into smaller florettes, dice olives into little pieces.

The Crust
Mix half a cup of butter and 2 cups of flower until mixture is uniform. Add salt, then use a fork to gradually mix in 6 tbsp of milk. Form dough mixture into a ball, then roll out and place in a well-greased pie or quiche pan. Cover dough with 1.5 cups of grated cheese.

The Filling
Sautee onion in olive oil for a couple of minutes. Add cavolo nero, with a little water, and cook for 2 minutes. Stir cauliflower into mix and cook until all is tender. Spread filling over cheese covered pastry. Beat 3 eggs and a cup of milk, season with salt, pepper and nutmeg. Pour over filling. Dress top with olives, and snippets of fresh herbs.

The Cooking and Finale
Bake in oven for 35-40 minutes at 190° C (375° F).
Serve with your favourite side dish of salad, or fries.

70

POTATO GATEAU

Serves 4

INGREDIENTS

1 kg potatoes
100-140 g diced ham
120 g smoked provola or mozzarella
Parmesan cheese
2 sprigs of parsley
2 eggs
Milk
Salt and pepper
Butter
Breadcrumbs

THE COOK

Mirella Castagna
Napoli, Italy

Retired Product Manager:
Oceania, Mexico,
North America
and the Caribbean Islands

TIP
If you don't like cooked potato skin, you can
peel the potatoes before or after boiling.

METHOD

Preparation
Wash unpeeled potatoes, chop parsley, beat egg. Dice provola/mozzarella. Pre-heat oven
to 180° C. Grease baking dish with butter. Boil unpeeled potatoes until soft; 30-40 minutes
depending on size. Mash hot cooked potatoes. Add beaten egg, diced ham, provola, half cup
of milk, 30 g of grated Parmesan, 20 g of butter and mix well. Season to taste, with salt
and pepper.
Grease bottom and sides of a baking dish with butter and sprinkle those areas
with breadcrumbs.

The Cooking
Spoon potato mixture evenly into baking tray, cover top with breadcrumbs
and a few knobs of butter.
Bake for 50 minutes.

The Finale
Let potato gateau cool before cutting and serving.
It's great with a fresh salad.

PUMPKIN STUFFED WITH MUSHROOMS

Serves 4

INGREDIENTS

2 mini hokkaido pumpkins (or small butternuts)
600 g mixed mushrooms (use your favourites)
1 onion
Cheddar cheese
Vegetable broth
Heavy (thickened) cream
Maple syrup
Balsamic vinegar
Butter
Salt, pepper
1 whole fresh nutmeg (or dried)
Flat parsley
Other vegetables: zucchini, beans, asparagus

THE COOK

Diané Ranck
Adelaide,
South Australia

Board Director:
Connective Creativity
and keen kayaker

METHOD

Preparation
Cut pumpkins in half. Scoop out seeds and a little flesh to create hollows.
Pre-heat oven to 180° C. Brush mushrooms clean and cut into quarters. Dice onion.
Grate 40 g of cheese.

The Pumpkin
Place pumpkins open-side up on a baking tray. Lightly salt fleshy tops. Bake for 30 minutes.

The Mushroom Ragout
In the meantime, stir fry onions and mushrooms together in 1 tbsp of butter. Add 1 tbsp of balsamic vinegar and 1 tbsp of maple syrup. Stir in 1 cup of stock/broth, a cup of cream and 2 tsp of grated nutmeg. Season with salt and pepper to taste. Cook over a low-medium heat for 5 minutes.

The Cooking
Fill pumpkin hollows with mushroom ragout. Dress generously with grated cheese.
Return to overn bake for 20-30 minutes.

The Finale
Dressed with parsley and serve with steamed beans, zucchini and asparagus.

STUFFED CAPSICUM WITH CURRY LEAF RICE

Serves 4

INGREDIENTS

2 red capsicums
Olive oil
30 g pine nuts
12 brown mushrooms
2 garlic cloves
Parsley
1 lime
Tahini
3 short cinnamon sticks
5 whole cloves
1 lemon
2 fresh curry leaves
1 cup basmati rice
60 g unsalted butter
Sea salt and ground pepper
Waxed paper and Aluminium foil

THE COOK

Susanne Stellberg
Frankfurt, Germany
and Voitsberg, Austria

**Senior Sales
and Marketing Manager:**
ULLIFINK Tourism
Marketing

METHOD

Preparation

Stuffed Capsicums: Cut capsicums in half length-wise. Remove inner sections and seeds. Dice mushrooms, crush garlic, chop parsley. Preheat oven to 200° C.

Lemon Curry Leaf Rice: Finely shave lemon zest (rind).

Cooking the Stuffed Capsicums

Place capsicum halves on a baking tray, drizzle with olive oil and bake for 10 minutes.
Meanwhile, fry pine nuts in a pan without oil until they are golden brown. Set aside.
Sauté mushrooms and garlic in 1 tbsp of olive oil until soft. Mix in pine nuts, juice of half a lime and 1 tbsp of tahini. Season with salt and pepper. Spoon mushroom mix into capsicum halves. Bake for another 15 minutes.

Cooking the Lemon and Curry Leaf Rice

In a large saucepan, put 3 cinnamon sticks, 5 cloves, lemon zest, curry leaves, 1 tsp salt and pepper and cover with 680 ml of water. Bring to the boil then remove saucepan from heat. Spread out 1 cup of rice in a baking dish (about 24 by 30 cm). Cover rice with aromatic boiled water, stir well then again spread to cover the dish.
Lay waxed paper over surface of the water, then cover the dish with aluminium foil. Cook in the oven for 25 minutes, then remove and leave to sit, covered, for 10 minutes.

The Finale

Just before serving, heat 60 g of butter in a small saucepan. Stir in 1 tbsp of lemon juice mix well. Pour this over hot rice and fluff it up with a fork. Transfer to a serving dish.
Serve stuffed capsicums with a sprinkle of fresh parsley.

VEGETABLE PIE WITH BLACK CABBAGE

Serves 4

INGREDIENTS

Half a black cabbage
(or purple cabbage or bunch of kale)
6 potatoes
2 white onions or leeks
2 eggs
Parmesan cheese
Robiola cheese or substitute
Basil – and/or your favourite fresh herbs
Ground cumin and/or chilli
1 garlic clove
Olive oil
Salt and ground black pepper

THE COOK

Paola Broggini
Milano, Italy
Product Specialist:
Alpitour

METHOD

Preparation
Peel and dice potatoes into small pieces. Finely chop cabbage. Tear or dice basil,
or other fresh herbs. Beat two eggs in a bowl, add cheeses and pinches of salt and pepper.
Preheat the oven to 180° C.

The Cooking
Boil potatoes for around 10 minutes. Heat 2 tbsp of olive oil in a large pan and toss in potatoes.
Season to taste with salt, pepper and ground cumin and/or chilli. Add cabbage and fresh herbs.
Stir for 5 minutes. Transfer vegetables to a baking pan. Pour egg and cheese mixture over
potato-cabbage mix. Bake in oven for about 35 minutes.

The Finale
Serve with other steamed vegetables or fresh salad.

CAULIFLOWER RICE WITH MUSHROOMS AND SEITAN

Serves 1-2

INGREDIENTS

Half a small cauliflower
50-70 g mushrooms
50 g of seitan
1 tsp Paprika
Half a glass of milk
Flour

THE COOK

Camilla Dalponte
Genoa, Italy
University student

TIPS

1) Seitan is a plant-based meat substitute high in protein, low in calories, carbs and fat.
2) It is made from gluten – its nickname is 'wheat meat' – so is not suitable for coeliacs or the gluten-intolerant.
3) You can use a different form of plant protein if you desire.
4) Cooking cream, instead of milk, makes it even tastier!

METHOD

Preparation
Use a blender to reduce half a cauliflower to small 'rice-like' pieces. Dice mushroom and chop seitan into squares.

The Cauliflower Rice
Add some oil into a pan and add cauliflower; season with salt to taste, add half a cup of water and simmer for about 10 minutes on medium heat. Do not let it dry out or burn.

The Seitan and Mushrooms
Heat oil in a second pan, add the seitan, salt, and cook for a few minutes on each side until golden brown. Put it aside. Repeat process for mushrooms, cooking them for 10 minutes or until brown. While they are cooking, mix half a tsp of flour in half a glass of milk. Add half this mix to mushrooms at 10-minute mark and continue cooking until mushrooms have absorbed most of the milk. Keep mixing to prevent milk from forming a skin.

The Finale
Add cooked mushrooms and seitan to cauliflower rice and mix everything together over medium heat adding remaining milk and paprika according to taste. Serve in a bowl for one; or as a side dish for two with a main meal.

BRUSSELS SPROUTS WITH APPLES AND CRANBERRIES

Serves 4

INGREDIENTS

350 g Brussels sprouts
Half a green apple
65 g cranberries
Olive oil
Salt and black pepper

TIPS

1) This is a perfect two-person side dish for any main meal, vegetarian or meat based; or a main meal for one.
2) Double the quantities to feed more people.

THE COOK

Camilla Dalponte
Genoa, Italy
University student

METHOD

Preparation
Cut sprouts in half. Peel and halve an apple.

The Cooking
Heat 1 tbsp of oil in a pan. Cook spouts on one side; season to taste with salt and pepper.
Stir in apples and cranberries. Add half a cup of water to cover them so that they soften for about 15 minutes or until the apples have flaked off, being careful not to burn them.

The Finale
Serve in bowls while hot.

FALAFEL

Serves 4

INGREDIENTS

1 cup dried chickpeas
1 onion
Fresh parsley
Fresh coriander
1 green capsicum
3 garlic cloves
Cumin
Cardamom
Salt and black pepper
Chickpea flour
Baking soda
Avocado oil
Tahini
Pita bread (or pockets) or Italian piadina
Salad mix: diced tomatoes, cucumber, lettuce

THE COOK

Nicolo Dalponte
Washington DC, USA

Consultant:
World Bank

METHOD

Preparation

Soak 1 cup of dried chickpeas overnight or at least 8 hours. Strain and rinse chickpeas.
Roughly chop onion, garlic, capsicum and the bunches of parsley and coriander.

The Mixture

Add the chickpeas, onion, garlic, capsicum, herbs, 1 tsp cumin, a half of cardamon to a food
processor. Blend on the pulse setting to a texture like coarse sand.
In a large bowl mix the falafel mix with 2 tbsp of chickpea flour, half a tsp of baking soda,
and season to taste with salt and pepper. Cover and chill in the fridge for 30-60 minutes.
Shape your falafel by hand into golfball-size shapes or fl atter patties.

The Cooking

Falafel can be deep fried, pan fried, or baked. Deep fry in 3 inches (7.5 cm) of avocado oil.
Or heat 2 tbsp of oil in a large pan and fry the falafel for 3 minutes each side. Or bake them
on an oiled over tray, at 200° C (400° F) for 25-30min, turning half way through.

The Finale

Falafel are best served immediately, when they're warm and crispy.
They're delicious in a wrap of pita, Italian piadina, or lettuce; with a diced salad (and fries!).
You can add them to, or serve with, a simple green salad. Or as a finger food to dip.
However you serve them, don't forget the all-important tahini sauce. (And/or hummus).

SIDES, SAUCES, SNACKS AND DIPS

AUSTRALIAN BEER DAMPER

Serves 2

INGREDIENTS

Self raising flour
250 ml beer
Salt
Sugar
Cooking oil

TIPS

1) You can add caraway seeds for flavour.
2) Damper tastes especially good when baked in a wood-fired stove, or an outside fire on the coals.

THE COOK

Diané Ranck
Adelaide,
South Australia

Board Director:
Connective Creativity
and keen kayaker

METHOD

Preparation
Lighly oil a round baking dish. Preheat oven to 190° C.

The Dough
In a large bowl, mix 2 cups of flour, 1 tsp each
of salt and sugar. Pour in 250 ml of good Aussie beer.
Mix using two knives until it becomes a wet dough.
Form dough into round shape and dust with flour
to stop dough from sticking.

The Cooking
Put dough into your round baking dish and bake
for 35-45 minutes.

Finale
Damper is best served warm. It's tasty just
as a bread or with soups, curries and stews.

BEER

TOMATO AND RED CAPSICUM CHUTNEY

Makes 4 jars

INGREDIENTS

1 1/2 kg tomatoes
2 white onions
2 large red capsicums
1 1/2 cups white vinegar
Fresh garlic
Fresh ginger
Salt and cracked pepper
10 whole cloves
1 1/4 cups sugar

METHOD

Preparation

First wash your jars and/or bottles in hot soapy water (or use dishwasher). To complete sterilisation place them in a cold oven, bring temperature to 120° C and leave for 30 minutes. Thinly slice onions, dice capsicums, crush 2 tbsp each of garlic and ginger. Use a blender to chop tomatoes.

The Cooking

In a large pan, place chopped tomatoes, vinegar, onions, capsicum, ginger, garlic and cloves. Season with salt and pepper and cook for 15 minutes, stirring all the time. Add sugar and boil until mixture has thickened to your desired consistency. About 15 minutes will give a thinnish sauce, boiling a little longer will produce thicker chutney.

The Finale

Bottle chutney in hot sterilised jars. Allow to cool and then seal jars. The chutney needs at least 3 weeks to mature before using. Refrigerate after opening. If stored unopened in a cool, dark place the chutney will keep for 12 months.

THE COOK

Rosalind Harries
Cairns, Australia

Owner:
Ros Harries Marketing

SPICED MANGO CHUTNEY

Makes 4 jars

INGREDIENTS

3 large mangoes
1 brown onion
Cider Vinegar
Raw sugar
Fresh root ginger
Salt
Yellow mustard seeds
Mixed spice
Chilli flakes
Curry powder
Ground cummin
Cloves

THE COOK

Maryanne Jacques
Cairns, Australia

Managing Director:
Cairns Discovery Tours

TIP
If you're only option is frozen mangoes,
this recipe needs 750 g of fruit.

METHOD

Preparation
Sterilise four large jars ready for storing chutney. Peel and slice mangoes. Dice onion. Peel and crush 150 g of ginger.

The Cooking
In a large saucepan, mix mango, onion and ginger with 50 ml of cider vinegar, 375 g of raw sugar and a pinch of salt. Add 1 tsp each of yellow mustard seeds and chilli flakes and half a tsp each of mixed spice, curry powder, ground cummin and ground cloves. Cook slowly, over a low heat, for 1 hour.

The Finale
When finished cooking, divide into sterilized jars. Seal jars while chutney is still hot.
Once chutney is cool, label jars and store in a cupboard. After you open a jar for use you then need to store it in the fridge.

SWEET FAROFA DE BANANA

Serves 4

INGREDIENTS

Manioc flour
1 large onion
3 garlic cloves
2 large bananas

Optional fruits and nuts

Apple,raisins, sultanas, dates, prunes, apricots
Walnuts, pine nuts, slivered almonds
Butter or cooking oil
Salt and black pepper
Chilli, cumin, cinnamon and coriander

The savoury version

2 rashers of thick cut bacon or 1 cup
of smoky sausage

THE COOKS

**Claudio Del Bianco
Owner:**
Del Bianco Travel

in collaboration with
Chef Simone Almeida
Rio/Brasil

Chef:
cookinrio.com

METHOD

Preparation

Chop onion into cubes. Finely dice garlic.
Peel and slice banana. Prepare fruit and nuts
you may be using: peel and dice apple, dice dates,
crush walnuts.

The Cooking

Heat 2 tbsp of butter or oil in a large pan,
add garlic and onion and cook until golden.
Mix in extra fruits and nuts you've chosen
(not banana) and continue to cook for a few
minutes (or until the apple is tender).
Season with salt and ground black pepper,
and add your favourite spices.
Stir in 400 g of manioc flour then toss and toast
until flour is golden and crunchy. Peel and slice
banana, stir in with other ingredients and turn off
heat. The banana and other ingredients should
be well coated.

The Finale

Serve as a side dish with other vegetarian dishes;
or with hearty stews, curries or barbecue.

*Farofa is the national side dish of Brazil
made primarily from toasted manioc flour,
which is made from cassava or yuca root,
combined with a host of ingredients.
The traditional savoury farofa recipe uses bacon
or other smokey sausage meat.
Our 'sweet' recipe here contains no meat
but, as a side dish, can be served with any
vegetarian or meat meal.*

TIPS

1) If you'd prefer to make the savoury version,
   simply fry the diced bacon then add to the
   manioc flour just after the onion and garlic.
2) You can still add banana and other fruits.

SPICED MOROCCAN CARROT DIP

Serves 4

INGREDIENTS

400 g carrots
Olive oil
1 tsp ground cumin
Pinch ground cinnamon
1 tsp paprika
2-3 cm piece fresh ginger
2 garlic cloves
1 tsp clear honey
Juice of 1 lemon
1 tbsp pine nuts
Green olives
Rucola (rocket)
Salt and pepper

THE COOK

Julie Weber
Benahavis, Spain

Director:
MTD Australia

METHOD

Preparation
Preheat oven to 200° C. Peel and thickly cut carrots. Grate ginger. Crush garlic.

The Cooking
Toss carrots with olive oil in a baking dish. Roast for 30-40 minutes until tender.
Remove from the oven and cool slightly. Pulse in a food processor and stir in cumin, cinnamon, paprika, ginger, garlic, honey and lemon juice. Season to taste.
Lightly toast pine nuts in a dry pan, until golden.

The Finale
Serve in bowls. Drizzle with olive oil and sprinkle with pine nuts. Garnish with green olives and rucola. Serve with toasted pita bread or crackers.

LEMON AND ROSEMARY CRISPY CRACKERS

Serves 4

INGREDIENTS

Dough
3/4 cup warm water
1 tsp active dry yeast
2 tsp sugar
2 cups all purpose flour
1 1/2 tbsp finely chopped rosemary
Grated zest from one lemon
2 tbsp extra virgin olive oil
1/4 tsp salt

Topping
1/4 cup extra virgin olive oil for brushing
Flaked or smoked sea salt
Ground black pepper

THE COOK

Morag Ritchie
London, UK

Australian Diplomat
/ Tourism sabbatical

METHOD

Preparation
Line baking trays with baking paper. Preheat oven to 180° C. Finely chop rosemary.
Grate zest of lemon.

The Dough
Combine 1 tsp of dry yeast and 1 tsp of sugar in 1 cup of warm water. Stir to dissolve and let sit
for about 5 minutes to activate yeast. In another bowl, combine 2 cups of flour and 2 tbsp
of olive oil with rosemary, lemon zest and a little salt.
When yeast is foamy, mix it thoroughly with flour mixture to form a ball of dough. (If it is too stiff,
add a little water; if too loose add a little flour.)
Knead dough for 6-8 minutes until smooth then place in a clean bowl brushed with olive oil.
Cover and set in a warm place to rise. When dough has doubled in size, punch down and turn
out on to a well-floured work surface. Knead for 30 seconds.

The Cooking
Pinch off around 40 walnut-sized pieces of dough.
Roll each piece until paper thin. Transfer to baking trays,
brush lightly with olive oil. Sprinkle with sea salt and pepper.
Bake for around 10 minutes,
rotating halfway through or until golden and crisp.

The Finale
Cool completely and store in an airtight container for up to 1 week.

SEED CRISP BREAD

Serves 4

INGREDIENTS

Coarse rye flour
Rolled oats
Sunflower seeds
Salt
Fennel seeds or dried rosemary
Water
Salt flakes

THE COOK

Susanne Larsson
Oslo, Norway

Travel Designer:
Blixen Tours

METHOD

Preparation
Pre-heat oven to 170 C. Line a baking tray with baking paper.

The Dough
Combine 250 ml of rye flour, 250 ml of rolled oats, 100 ml sunflower seeds, 1 tsp of salt
and 1.5 tsp of fennel seeds (or 2 tsp of rosmary) with 300 ml of water. Using wet hands,
press and roll dough out as thinly as possible on the oven tray, making sure you cover the whole
sheet of paper. Score or cut dough into evenly sized pieces. Sprinkle with salt flakes.

The Cooking
Bake for 1 hour or until crisp bread is completely hard. Leave to cool on a rack.

The Finale
Break into pieces and store in a dry place at room temperature.

TARALLINI PUGLIESI

Serves 4

INGREDIENTS

Plain flour
Salt
Water
Dry white wine
Baking powder

THE COOK

Marina Fidele
Milan, Italy

Travel Agent:
Mondo for You

METHOD

Preparation
Pre-heat oven to 180° C. Prepare a large baking sheet lined with baking paper.

The Tarallini Dough
In a large bowl, mix 90 ml of wine, 50 ml of water, 8 g baking powder and tsp of salt. Add 400 g flour, a little at a time, while mixing with a spatula. Knead tarallini dough with your hands until it's soft and elastic. Divide dough in 4 equal pieces. Roll out each piece and cut in pieces of about 12-14gr each.
Take each small piece and roll it out to a rope, join the end and press lightly so they stick together to form a circle. Put all tarallini on the baking sheet.

The Cooking
Bake in oven for about 30 minutes, turning tarallini over after 15 minutes so they cook well on both sides.

CHEESE AND ROCKET SCONES

Serves 6-8

INGREDIENTS

Self-raising flour
Baking powder
Salt
Cayenne pepper
Rocket leaves
Tasty cheese
Chilled cream
Chilled soda water
Butter
Fresh tomatoes

THE COOK

Rosalind Harries
Cairns, Australia

Owner:
Ros Harries Marketing

TIPS

1) These scones freeze really well.
2) They can either be reheated in a microwave or partly defrosted (naturally or microwave) then cut in half and popped in a toaster.

METHOD

Preparation

Preheat oven to 200° C. Line a baking tray with baking paper. Grate 200 g of tasty cheese. Finely chop 75 g (three handfuls) of rocket.

The Dough

In a mixing bowl combine 4 cups of flour, 1.5 tsp of baking powder, 1 tsp of salt and a pinch of cayenne. Then mix in chopped rocket and cheese. In a separate bowl or jug, combine 1 cup of cream and 1 cup of soda water. Make a well in the centre of the dry ingredients and pour in the liquid. Mix with a spatual until just combined. Alternatively, use a food processor to combine all dry ingeredients, then add soda and cream and pulse only 3-4 times. Turn scone dough out onto a lightly floured surface and pat into a rough rectangle about 4 cm thick. Cut into 12-16 pieces and place on prepared baking tray.

The Cooking

Bake for 15-18 minutes – until scones are puffed and golden and they bounce back when pressed.

The Finale

Serve hot with butter and sliced tomatoes or other favourite toppings.

CRUMBED PUMPKIN SURPRISE

Serves 4

INGREDIENTS

Butternut pumpkin
Flour
Breadcrumbs
1 egg
Salt and pepper
Paprika
Parsley
50 g Pumpkin Seeds
Sugar
Sunflower oil

THE COOK

Carmen Laurella
Italy

Sales Manager UK/Europe:
Luxury Hotels Australia

TIP

Crumbed pumpkin is a great starter, side dish or even a snack.

METHOD

Preparation
Peel, rinse and dry eight thick (circular) slices of pumpkin. In a flat bowl, beat one egg, add finely-diced parsley and season with salt, pepper and paprika. Prepare two other flat bowls, one with 200 g flour and one with 200 g of breadcrumbs.

The Cooking
Dip both sides of each pumpkin slice in flour, then egg mix, then breadcrumbs. Heat some sunflower oil in a large pan and fry crumbed pumpkin on medium. Turn them 2-3 times until golden brown. Put aside. In a fresh pan, heat 1 tbsp and 4 tbsp of sugar, then toss in 50 g of pumpkin seeds and stir until caramelised. Spread cooked seeds onto a baking tray and crush them with a fork.

The Finale
Once crumbed pumpkin slices are cooked, transfer briefly to paper towel to drain the excess oil and then to a serving dish or individual plates. Dress slices with the toasted pumpkin seeds.

Cooking is indeed a form of art.
It requires creativity and passion.
Being an artistic soul, every time I cook
it is like every time I draw.
The imagination takes over as well as the
love of creating.
One Sunday for lunch, I created this dish.

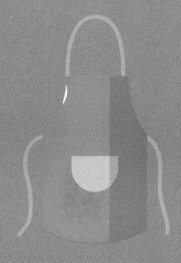

BUSH
AND BEACH

IKA MATA: RAW FISH IN COCONUT CREAM

Serves 2

INGREDIENTS

350 g fish fillets
(tuna, mullet, parrot fish, trevally
or any fine flesh fish)
1 cup lemon or lime juice
1 cup thick coconut cream
1 green onion
2 tomatoes
2 carrots
Salt

THE COOK

Jacopo Dozzo
Rarotonga, Cook Islands

**Destination Mgt
Cook Islands - Manager:**
Turama Pacific
Travel Group

METHOD

Preparation
Cut fish fillets into 1.5 cm pieces. Sprinkle with salt and leave for few minutes. Pour 1 cup of lemon (or lime) juice over fish. The pieces must be just covered. Leave in refrigerator at least 2 hours until fish is white. The time taken to whiten depends on the fish and acidity of the citrus fruit. Meanwhile finely dice onion, tomatoes and carrots and mix together. When fish is white, strain off juice and squeeze excess moisture by pressing gently in a strainer. Transfer to a serving plate. Pour 1 cup of thick coconut cream over fish.

The Finale
Garnish your fish with onion, tomatoes and carrots. Serve well chilled.

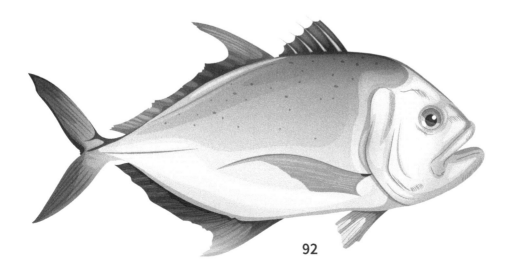

SAMOAN FISH SALAD OKA A'I

Serves 4-6

INGREDIENTS

450 g fresh tuna
65 ml fresh lemon or lime juice
1 small onion
2 spring onions
2 tomatoes
1 cucumber
1 cup coconut milk
Salt

TIPS

1) You can use any fish you like, just make sure it is really fresh.
2) If you like extra spicy hot, add a minced serrano chilli.

THE COOK

Sebastian Sarrasin
London, UK
Account Director:
Representation Plus

METHOD

Preparation

Dice onion, slice spring onion and tomatoes. Peel, de-seed and dice cucumber. Cut your fish into bite size pieces. Place in a bowl and cover with freshly squeezed citrus juice. Marinate for about 10 minutes. The citrus juice cooks the diced fish quickly. Drain citrus juice from fish, mix in the vegetables. Add coconut milk and salt to taste.

The Finale

Refrigerate for about an hour to let all the flavours meld together and serve.

CHOCOLATE AND WATTLESEED BISCUITS

Serves 4-6

INGREDIENTS

100 g butter
65 g roasted wattleseed
65 g white sugar
1 egg
128 g plain flour
96 g cocoa
96 g brown sugar
1 tsp vanilla extract
100 g chocolate chips

TIP

If you can't source wattleseed, you can use granulated coffee instead.

THE COOK

Dale Tilbrook
Perth,
Western Australia

Director:
Dale Tilbrook
Experiences
Indigenous Tourism
Operator

METHOD

Preparation
Line a baking tray with baking paper. Preheat oven to 180° C.

The Biscuit Mix
Place half the wattleseed (35 g) in a bowl and just cover with hot water. Soak for 5 minutes. Soften butter and mix into soaked wattleseed. Set aside for 10 minutes. Stir the white sugar into wattleseed butter, then mix in 1 beaten egg. Next mix in the flour, cocoa, brown sugar and vanilla extract, then fold in chocolate chips.

The Cooking
Place tbsp-sized balls of biscuit mix, evenly spaced, on baking tray. Flatten slightly.
Sprinkle with the rest of the wattleseed. Bake for 8-10 minutes.

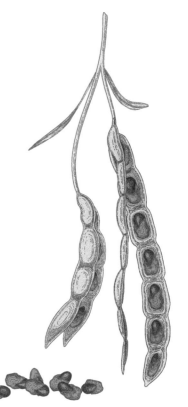

PIZZA AL PASTOR

Serves 2

INGREDIENTS

500 g pork fillet
2 tbsp rice bran, or vegetable oil
2 garlic cloves
4 tbsp kecap manis
1 cup pineapple pieces
1 cup coriander (cilantro)
3-4 Chipotle chillies
1 cup tomatillo salsa (green)
4 spring onions chopped
Pizza base of your choice

THE COOK

Andrew Dwyer
Jamieson Victoria,
Australia

Owner:
Diamantina Touring
Company

METHOD

Preparation
Dice pork, garlic, chillies and spring onions. Preheat the oven to 250 C.

The Topping
Heat oil in a wok. Add garlic and stir for a couple of seconds. Add pork and kecap manis and stir fry until cooked through. Set aside.

The Pizza
Spread your pizza base with tomatillo salsa evenly, as you would a passata. Scatter base with cooked pork, coriander, chillies, spring onions and pineapple. Bake for 10 minutes.

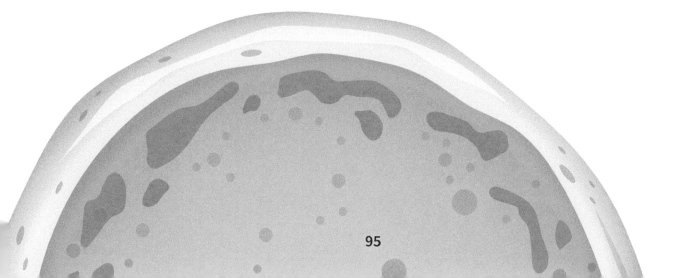

GRANOLA

Serves 4-6

INGREDIENTS

4 cups rolled oats
2 tbsp pure coconut palm sugar
150 ml grape nectar (or honey)
2 tbsp manuka honey
(optional for extra sweetness)
8 shots espresso coffee
33 g cocoa powder
1 tbsp ground roasted wattleseed
2 vanilla beans, seeds scrapped
200 ml orange juice
35 ml sweet almond oil
128 ml extra virgin olive oil
128 g chopped almonds
128 g flaked coconut
64 g (Australian) dried muscatel grapes
64 g dried fig halves
64 g dried cranberries or air-dried cherry

THE COOK

Andrew Dwyer
Jamieson Victoria,
Australia

Owner:
Diamantina Touring
Company

METHOD

Preparation

Combine all ingredients – except fruit, almonds and coconut. The oats should be well-coated and slightly moist. Spread mixture out evenly on a large tray and top with almonds and coconut flakes.

Bake in oven until mixture crisps up. The longer you cook and the lower the temperature the better; 80 C for a couple of hours is good. Remove and, while still slightly warm, toss through dried fruit.

The Finale

You should have clusters of oats. Serve with milk.

WALKABOUT MUD CRAB

Serves 2

INGREDIENTS

1 mud crab (800 g – 1 kg)
3 garlic cloves
3 chillies
33 ml brown vinegar
2 pinches of salt
1 tbsp coconut oil
1 tbsp butter
1 lime

TIPS

1) To get real Australian mud crab you'll need to go out on Country with Juan.
2) Substitute with local crab if you can't get to Australia right now.

THE COOK

Juan Walker
Tropical North Queensland

Indigenous Tourism Operator:
Walkabout Cultural Adventures

METHOD

Preparation
Finely dice garlic and chillies. Break crab in to pieces (remove claws with hands, cut body up with a knife).

The Cooking
Heat coconut oil and butter in a wok. Add garlic and chillies stir fry until the garlic browns.
Pour in the vinegar and add the crab (in pieces). Keep turning the crab until it's cooked through.

The Finale
Add salt, toss, squeeze lime and serve.

FIJIAN COCONUT CHOCOLATE BROWNIE

Serves 4-6

INGREDIENTS

250 g butter
500 g brown sugar
125 g cocoa
4 eggs
1 tsp vanilla extract
100 g desiccated coconut

TIP

This recipe is from Taste Fiji, a family run café in Nadi and one of my favourite eateries in Fiji.

THE COOK

Conny Schütz
Munich, Germany

Market Manager Germany:
Tourism Fiji

METHOD

Preparation
Line a 24 cm square cake tin with baking paper. Preheat oven to 160° C (fan-forced) or 180° C (conventional).

The Batter
In a small saucepan gently melt butter and sugar. Stir in cocoa and mix well. Use a blender to beat eggs and vanilla until light and fluffy. Combine chocolate mixture and coconut to eggs and mix well.

The Cooking
Turn batter into the prepared cake tin. Bake for 40 minutes. The centre will still be a little soft when cooked.

The Finale
Allow to cool and then cut into 16 pieces. Enjoy!

CHICKEN FA'FA'

Serves 4-6

INGREDIENTS

6 chicken breasts
1 bunch of fāfā (taro leaves)
2 onions
1 piece of ginger
1 lime
1 litre of broth
Coconut milk
Salt and pepper
Olive Oil

TIP
If taro leaves are not available use spinach leaves.

THE COOK

Gabriele Cavallotti
Italy

Account Manager:
Tahiti Tourisme

METHOD

Preparation
Boil fāfā leaves in plenty of lightly salted water for an hour. Drain well. Cut chicken breasts into small pieces. Peel and thinly slice the onions and ginger.

The Cooking
Heat 3 tbsp of oil in a large pan or wok. Stir fry the chicken pieces, with salt and pepper to taste, for 10 minutes.
Add the fāfā leaves, the stock and the lime juice.
Mix well, turn the heat right down and simmer for an hour.

The Finale
Stir the coconut milk through before serving.

BANANA PO'E

Serves 4-6

INGREDIENTS

6 – 8 bananas
Banana leaves
150 – 200 g cassava starch
50 – 75 g sugar
Milk from a grated coconut

Pre-heat oven to medium

TIPS

1) If you don't have banana leaves you can use aluminium foil.
2) Alternatives to cassava starch include arrowroot, tapioca flour, almond flour, coconut flour, chickpea flour and rice flour.

THE COOK

Gabriele Cavallotti
Italy

Account Manager:
Tahiti Tourisme

METHOD

Preparation
Peel bananas and cook them in a little water. Drain and mash them. In a bowl, mix banana purée with starch and sugar.
Proportions: for every two cups of bananas use 128 g of starch and 50 g of sugar.
Pour mixture onto a lightly oiled banana leaf.

The Cooking
Bake in oven at medium temperature for 30-40 minutes.

The Finale
Add coconut milk before serving.

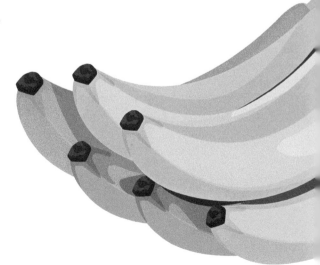

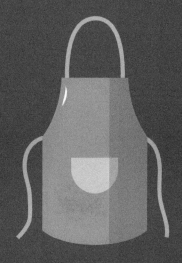

SWEETS
AND CAKES

HEAVEN TIRAMISÙ (TIRAMISÙ IN LOVE)

Serves 4-6

INGREDIENTS

1st Cream:

2 eggs
2 tbsp white sugar
1 kg mascarpone cream
200 g chocolate chips

2nd Cream:

2 eggs
80 g white sugar
80 g icing sugar

Other:

400 g of Pavesini biscuits (ladyfingers)
3 Espresso coffee shots (approx. 90ml)
Cocoa powder to dust
Strawberries, almonds & pistachios for decorating

TIPS

1) Do not over-mix the cream.
2) Dip biscuits only when coffee is cold.
3) Dip biscuits quickly else they will go soggy.
4) Fridge for minimum 2 hrs, overnight better.
5) Pavesini biscuits givs a more delicate flavour but use biscuits you have available.

THE COOK

Carmen Laurella
Italy

Sales Manager UK/Europe:
Luxury Hotels Australia

" *Tiramisù, the favourite Italian life love, is one of my preferences. Over the years I have created many combinations and this is one of my favourites. For those who love and are in love with chocolate, here is my "Tiramisù in Love", dedicated to all the lovers in the world. I also make mini Tiramisù with the same procedure.* "

METHOD

Preparation

Make the espresso coffee first and let it cool.

First Cream: Separate egg whites and yolks. Add sugar to the egg yolks and whip until soft peaks form (after two minutes of whipping, egg yolks will start to thicken). Mix egg whites to egg yolks. Add mascarpone and mix until well blended. Add chocolate chips to cream and put aside.

Second Cream: (Basically the same mixture I use to make meringues.) Separate egg whites and yolks. Add the sugar to the whites, beat with electric mixer until peaks form. Add icing sugar and use a spoon for turning the mixture from the bottom to the top.

The Making

Dip each ladyfinger biscuit into the coffee (do not soak too much), arrange to fill base of a dish. Spread layer of first cream mixture. Arrange another layer of biscuits. Spread layer of second cream mixture. Repeat layers and cover the top with a generous amount of cocoa powder. Decorate the top with strawberries, pistachios, almonds and chocolate.

The Finale

Place in fridge for minimum of 2 hours before serving.

APPLE AND PECAN CAKE

Serves 4

INGREDIENTS

2 large cooking apples
Pecan nuts
Sugar
Plain flour
Bicarb soda
Cinnamon
Allspice
Salt
2 eggs
Butter
Cream
Vanilla essence

THE COOK

Diana Jaquillard
Adelaide, Australia

Retired graphic designer

Foundation Board:
The Helpman Academy

TIPS

1) When you make this delicious and simple cake, your house will be filled with the divine spicy aroma of the baked apples, allspice and cinnamon!

METHOD

Preparation
Lightly grease a 20 cm square cake tin, line bottom with baking paper. Preheat the oven to 180° C. Peel, core and cut 2 apples into small chunks. Roughly chop a cup of pecans.

The Cooking
Mix chopped apples with 1 cup of sugar and set aside. In another bowl, sift together 1.5 cups of flour with 1 tsp each of bicarb soda, cinnamon and allspice. Add a pinch of salt and mix in chopped pecans. Melt 125 g of butter, allow to cool, then beat two eggs into it. Stir the egg-butter mixture into spiced flour, then add apples and mix well. Spoon mixture into prepared cake tin. Bake for 45-55 minutes. Test with a skewer after 45 minutes to see if it comes out clean.

The Finale
Serve with cream whipped with a touch of sugar and vanilla essence.

BANANA BREAD

Serves 2

INGREDIENTS

3 overripe bananas
Flour
Baking powder
Baking soda
Salt
Butter
Brown sugar
2 eggs
Milk
Vanilla sugar or vanilla essence

TIP

It's always best to use overripe bananas
in and banana cake recipe. Even the brown
ones you may not ordinarily eat raw
are perfect.

THE COOK

Sabine Schamburger
Trier, Germany
Product Manager:
Boomerang Reisen

METHOD

Preparation

Grease a baking/cake tin with butter and a sprinkle of breadcrumbs or line it with baking paper.
Preheat oven to 180° C. Beat 2 eggs. Measure out 125 ml of milk. Mash 2-3 bananas with a fork.

The Cooking

Beat 175 g of butter with 200 g of sugar until fluffy. Add in beaten eggs and 1 sachet of vanilla
sugar or 1 tsp of vanilla essence. In a large bowl mix 275 g of flour with half a tsp of baking soda,
1.5 tsp of baking powder and a pinch of salt. Stir into the flour mix half the butter-egg mixture
then half the milk. Mix well, then repeat. Finally, fold in the mashed banana. Pour mixture into
your baking tin. Bake for about 60 minutes on lowest oven rack.

The Finale

This banana bread tastes delicious straight from the oven. If you leave it for a day it becomes
even sweeter.

COUNTRY WOMEN'S ASSOCIATION (CWA) SCONES

Serves 4

INGREDIENTS

Self raising flour
Cold cream
Lemonade
Salt
Your favourite jam
Extra cream for whipping

THE COOK

Maryanne Jacques
Cairns, Australia

Managing Director:
Cairns Discovery Tours

TIP
Adding mascaropone – or similar soft cheese – softens the overall texture and lessens the strong flavour.

METHOD

Preparation
Pre-heat oven to 220° C. Lightly grease a baking tray with butter or line with baking paper.

The Cooking
Sift 5 cups of flour, three times, into a bowl. Add a pinch of salt as you sift. Fold in 300 ml of cold cream and 300 ml of lemonade. Keep folding mixture until flour is well mixed into a doughy texture.
Roll dough out, to about 2 cm thick, onto a lightly floured surface. Cut into shapes of about 6 cm diameter, and brush each one with milk. Arrange scones onto your baking tray and pop them into the oven for 10 minutes or until golden brown.

The Finale
Scones are always best served hot. Enjoy with your favourite jam and whipped cream.

BACI DI DAMA

Serves 4

INGREDIENTS

Butter (soft)
Almond flour
Plain flour
Sugar
Salt
1 egg
Dark chocolate
Milk

TIPS

1) Use kitchen gloves to avoid blackening your fingers.
2) Double the number of artichokes to feed more people.

THE COOK

Luca Dal Cookie
Genova, Italy

Scientist

METHOD

Preparation

Dice 300 g of butter and leave until it's at room temperature. Separate one egg white.
When you're ready to start cooking, preheat oven to 180° C. Line a baking tray with baking paper.

The Dough

In a large bowl combine soft butter with 300 g of sugar. Sift 300 g of almond flour together with 300 g of plain flour, then fold butter and sugar into flour mix. Mix egg white with a pinch of salt and blend into flour mixture.
The end result should be a firm maleable dough. Transfer it to a flat surface and shape into a compact square. Wrap in plastic wrap and cool in fridge for about 3 hours to stabilise it.

The Cooking

Roll your dough out on a lightly-floured surface to 1 cm thick, then cut into 2 cm squares.
Roll each piece into balls, then gently press each onto the baking to form half-spheres.
Bake for 10-15 min or until golden. While they're baking, melt 200 g of dark chocolate, stir in a tbsp of butter and a little milk to form an even chocolate cream.

The Finale

Once baked, turn half of the baci upside down and cover flat side with chocolate cream. Pair each one with another half-sphere. Baci di dama – or lady's kisses – are ideal with fresh-brewed coffee.

BAUMKUCHEN = PYRAMID CAKE

INGREDIENTS

Cake
375 g butter plus extra for greasing
375 g white sugar
12 g vanilla sugar
3 eggs plus 6 egg yolks
4 egg whites
2 tbsp rum (optional)
225 g plain flour
150 g starch
4.5 tsp baking powder

Coating
250 g milk or dark chocolate
125 g apricot jam
1 tbsp sugar
3 tbsp water
Marzipan for decoration

THE COOK

Eva Seller
Frankfurt, Germany

**Regional Manager
– Continental Europe:**
Tourism Australia

METHOD

Preparation
Pre-heat oven to 175° C. Whisk butter until frothy, mix in white sugar, vanilla sugar, whole eggs, egg yolks and rum. In a separate bowl, mix flour, baking powder and starch together. Stir into the butter mixture slowly until well combined.
Beat egg whites until stiff, stir into mixture slowly so you don't lose the air, until fully incorporated.

TIP
Wrap cooled cake in tin foil tightly, let sit for around 3 weeks to allow flavours to infuse. Enjoy it in thin slices.

The Cooking
Grease 26 cm springform pan with extra butter. Add 3 tbsp cake mixture to pan and bake for 10 minutes to make first layer. Add another 3 tbsp of cake mixture on top, bake for 10 minutes. Repeat process until mixture is used up or the pan is full. You should get 8 to 9 layers.
Meanwhile, add apricot jam, sugar and water to small saucepan, bring to boil and stir for a minute or two until jam and sugar are dissolved.
When the last layer is baked, carefully take cake out of the pan. Brush or spoon jam sauce over the top and side. Pour remaining sauce evenly over the top and let it soak in to the cake. Put cake on a wire rack and let it cool completely.

The Finale
Melt chocolate to make a thick sauce. Coat cooled cake all over with the sauce and decorate with marzipan.

BUCHTELN

Serves 2

INGREDIENTS

Fresh yeast
Sugar
Milk
2 eggs
1 vanilla bean
1 lemon
Salt
Flour
Jam – your favourite
Butter
Powdered sugar

THE COOK

Michela Aldegheri
Verona, Italy

Manager Director:
Fiji Time Viaggi

METHOD

Preparation
In a bowl, mix 140 ml of warm milk with 60 g of sugar and 25 g of fresh yeast. Set aside for
20 minutes to rise. De-seed vanilla bean. Grate zest of 1 lemon. Melt 40 g of butter. Beat 2 eggs.

The Dough
To risen yeast, add 400 g of flour, vanilla seeds, lemon zest, pinch of salt, butter and the beaten
eggs. Mix well and let stand for 30 minutes at room temperature. On a lightly-floured surface,
roll out dough to a 1 cm thick sheet. Use round cutter to make discs with a diameter of 6 to 8 cm.
Place a dollop of jam in the centre of each, then close the sides to form a small ball. Brush top
of each with melted butter. Place buchteln on a buttered pan and let stand for for another
30 minutes at room temp.

The Cooking
Cook buchteln for 30 min at 180° C.

The Finale
Dust buchteln with powdered sugar and serve warm.

BULGARIAN YOGURT CAKE

Serves 4

INGREDIENTS

Butter
Sugar
Vanilla essence
4 eggs
Plain yoghurt
Baking soda
Plain flour
Whole wheat flour
Walnuts
Prunes
Apricots
Raisins

METHOD

Preparation

Chop 250 g of walnuts, and 125 g each
of prunes, apricots and raisins. Pre-heat oven
to 180° C (350° F). Grease bundt or baking tin.

The Batter

In a large bowl, cream 250 g of soft butter
and 1 cup of sugar until light and fluffy.
Beat in 1 tsp of vanilla essence. Then add one
egg at a time, mixing each well. In a separate
bowl, combine 300 g of yoghurt with 1 tsp of
baking soda. In another bowl, combine 425 g
of plain flour and 165 g of whole wheat flour.
Alternating between them, mix the flour
and yoghurt combinations into cream mixture.
When it's all well blended, fold in walnuts
and dried fruits.

The Cooking

Pour mixture into bundt and bake for about
45 minutes, or until toothpick inserted
in middle comes out clean.

The Finale

If desired, top with a simple powdered sugar
and water icing.

THE COOK

Mary Retzler
Rome, Italy

**Marketing
and PR Coordinator:**
Cathay Pacific

TIPS

1) You can use a bundt pan or an ordinary
   9" x 13" cake tin
2) Other yoghurt fl avours can be used:
   lemon, strawberry; whatever you have
   or need to use up
3) Other nuts and dried fruits can also
   be used.

BUNDT CAKE

Serves 2

INGREDIENTS

Self-raising flour
Sugar
Unsalted butter
4 eggs
Vanilla sugar
Vanilla essence

TIPS

1) My daughter and I love cooking this together and, of course, she loves licking the bowl after.
2) You use plain flour instead of self-raising but remember to add 1 tsp of baking powder.
3) This recipe is not too sweet so you can add icing if you like. But it's lovely without.

THE COOK

Petra Steinig
Brisbane, Australia
Managing Director:
Travel Insiders

METHOD

Preparation
Separate white and yolks of four eggs. Preheat oven to 180° C.

The Batter
Melt 250 g butter in a pot. Make sure it doesn't boil. Use 2 tbsp of butter to grease the bundt. Beat egg white with 1 tsp of vanilla sugar until it's stiff, and put aside. In large bowl, mix 250 g of sugar, the 4 yolks, 2 tbsp of water and beat until foamy. Stir 300 g of flour into egg mix, then add melted butter and 1 tsp vanilla essence and beat until it all forms a smooth dough. Fold beaten egg white into dough with a large spoon and stir to make smooth.

The Cooking
Pour mix into bundt cake tin. Bake for 45 minutes.

The Finale
Let cake cool down for about 20 minutes before gently shaking tin to release cake onto a plate. It's lovely served with whipped cream.

CARMEN'S SWEET INDULGENCE

Serves 4

INGREDIENTS

Manitoba flour (or wheat flour for bread)
Plain Flour
Fresh yeast
Milk (at room temp)
Butter
Sugar
Salt
3 eggs
Ricotta
1 lemon

TIPS

1) Adding mascaropone – or similar soft cheese – softens the overall texture and lessens the strong flavour.

THE COOK

Carmen Laurella
Italy

Sales Manager UK/Europe:
Luxury Hotels Australia

METHOD

The Dough

Melt 50 g of butter and set aside to cool. Sift 350 g of plain and 150 g of 'Manitoba' flour into a bowl. Mix in 2 tsp of yeast, 300 ml of milk, and 60 g of sugar, with a fork; then continue by hand to form an even dough. Add in melted butter, a tsp of salt, and knead again. Then work dough, on a lightly oiled surface, until it's smooth and elastic. Place dough in a lightly-buttered bowl, cover with cling film, and rest it for an hour. Once dough has doubled in size, turn it out onto a lightly-floured surface and punch down on it to remove excess air. Divide in to about 18 circular rolls. Arrange them 2 cm apart on a tray lined with baking paper. Beat 1 egg with 20 ml of milk and use to brush the tops of the rolls. Set aside for 30 minutes to rise. They should double in size again. Meanwhile pre-heat your oven to 180° C.

The Cooking

Bake the rolls for about 25 minutes, or until golden. Transfer them to a wire rack to cool.

The Finale

While your rolls are baking, prepare lemon cream filling by combining 500 g of ricotta, 50 g of sugar, 1 egg plus a yolk, and zest of 1 lemon. Alternatively you can spread your rolls with Nutella (my favourite) or your choice of jam. Or my 'sweet indulgence' are also perfect dinner rolls, spread with butter, to accompany any soup or hearty stew and are also tasty with a cream cheese spread.

SWEDISH SEMLOR

Serves 4

INGREDIENTS

Butter
Milk
Fresh yeast (for sweet dough)
Crushed cardamom
(or the grated peel of 1 orange)
Salt
Sugar
Plain flour
1 egg
Marzipan
100 ml milk
Whipping cream
Icing sugar

THE COOK

Susanne Larsson
Oslo, Norway
Travel Designer:
Blixen Tours

METHOD

The Dough
Crumble 50 g of yeast in a bowl, add 1 tsp of cardamom (or the grated orange peel).
Melt 100 g butter, add 300 ml of milk and heat to 37° C. Stir warmed milk into yeast. Add half tsp of salt, 85 g of sugar and 550 g of flour. Use a food processor (15 minutes) to work mixture into dough. Set aside for 40 minutes to rise to twice its size in the bowl. Roll dough out to 3 cm thick on a lightly-floured surface and cut into even pieces. Shape pieces into bun shapes, place them on a greased baking tray and, again, leave buns for about an hour to rise to twice their size.

The Cooking
Brush buns with beaten egg. Bake on a low rack at 225° C for 8–10 minutes until golden.

The Finale
When buns are cool, cut tops off, scoop 2 tsp of cake from centre of each and crumble those centres all together in a bowl.
Grate 200 g marzipan into crumbles. Stir 100 ml of milk in to make a creamy mass.
Fill hollow buns with this mixture. Whip 300 ml cream and spoon it over filling.
Replace top on the bun and dust with icing sugar.

CARROT AND WALNUT CAKE

Serves 6-8

INGREDIENTS

160 g plain flour
Half a tsp baking powder
Half a tsp bicarbonate of soda
1 tsp ground cinnamon
Quarter of a tsp ground cloves
1 large free-range egg
1 free-range egg yolk
200 g sunflower oil
270 g caster sugar
50 g walnuts, chopped
50 g desiccated coconut
135 g carrot, roughly grated
2 free-range egg whites
a pinch of salt

Icing:
175 g cream cheese, at room temp
70 g unsalted butter
35 g icing sugar
25 g honey
30 g walnuts, chopped & lightly toasted

THE COOK

Sandra Feustel
Sydney, Australia

General Manager Product & Client Relations:
Pan Pacific Travel AustraliA

TIP

This is a very fluffy version of a carrot cake, not the usual dense one. It's really the only cake I can bake, but someone said it was the best birthday cake they ever had.

METHOD

Preparation
Grate the carrot, chop the walnuts; lightly whisk one whole egg with the yolk of a second; separate the whites and yolks from another 2 eggs. Sift the flour, baking powder, bicarbonate of soda and spices together. Beat the sunflower oil and caster sugar in an electric mixer for a minute. Then, on a low speed, add the beaten egg. Next, mix in 50 g walnuts, coconut and carrot and blend for 30 seconds; then add the sifted dry ingredients. Transfer the cake batter to a large bowl. In a separate bowl, whisk the three egg whites and a pinch of salt, until firm. Fold the egg whites into the batter. Don't over mix; there should be white streaks.

The Cooking
Pour the batter into a spring-form greased cake tin. Bake at 170 C for an hour. Cover with foil if the top is cooking faster than the centre. When done allow the cake to cool then remove from the tin.

The Icing Finale
Using a mixer, blend the butter, icing sugar and honey until light and airy. Separately, beat the cream cheese until light and smooth. Fold the two together then spread waves of the icing on top of the cake. Sprinkle with (lightly toasted) walnuts.

CHOCOLATE CHERRY TART

Serves 4-6

INGREDIENTS

300 g packet dark chocolate shortcrust pastry
(or just google a chocolate shortcrust recipe)
265 g morello cherries in syrup
55 g caster sugar
200 g red glacé cherries
3 tsp arrowroot
70 g shredded coconut
150 g dark chocolate
2 tbsp pure (thin) cream

TIP

Both the pastry and the filling can be made a few days ahead and put together on the day of serving. If you're doing this keep the chocolate to last so that it is nice a glossy when you serve it.

THE COOK

Cherie Glare
Cairns, Australia
Sales Development Manager:
The CaPTA Group

METHOD

Preparation
Thaw pastry, dice the glacé cherries and chocolate. Preheat oven to 180° C.

The Base
Line a 35cm x 12cm loose-bottomed tart pan with pastry. Prick it with a fork, chill for 10 minutes. Cover pastry with baking paper and fill with pastry weights (or uncooked rice). Bake for 10 minutes then remove baking paper and weights. Return to oven for 5-7 minutes until pastry is crisp on the surface. Allow to cool.

The Filling
Drain morello cherries reserving 125 ml of syrup.
Mix cherries, caster sugar, glacé cherries and syrup in a saucepan, bring to a simmer and cook for 5 minutes. Remove 2 tbsp of the liquid, mix with arrowroot into a smooth paste, then return to the pan, stir and simmer for 1 minute, or until thick. Pour into a bowl, then chill for 20 minutes. Fold coconut into the cherry mixture, then pour into tart case. Refrigerate for an hour. Combine chocolate and cream in a small bowl and melt in microwave. Cool to room temperature, then spread over the tart.

The Finale
Run a fork through the chocolate to create decorative lines. Cut into slices and serve.

QUICK COFFEE MOUSSE WITH BAILEYS

Serves 4

INGREDIENTS

500 ml fresh cold cream
2 cups of cold mocha coffee
1 tbsp of instant coffee
1 tbsp of Baileys
3 tbsp of icing sugar
Unsweetened cocoa powder

TIPS

The cream and the tools used to whip should be very cold (from the refrigerator).
You can substitute scotch whiskey for Baileys; and cocoa powder for coffee.

THE COOK

Elena Paracchi
Torino, Italy

Owner:
catviaggi.net

METHOD

Preparation
Whip cream with an electric mixer until it begins to take shape. Add instant coffee, Baileys, mocha coffee and icing sugar. Resume blending until you get a very thick and foamy cream. Transfer mixture into your dessert glasses.

The Finale
Use a sieve to sprinkle each mousse with unsweetened cocoa.

QUICK AND EASY CUPCAKES

Makes 12

INGREDIENTS

60 g butter
75 g caster sugar
110 g flour
4 g baking powder
60 ml milk
1 egg
Flavours – see Tips

TIPS

Some flavour ideas:

1) Chocolate: add 2-3 tbsp chocolate powder. Add chocolate chips to the batter of each cupcake before baking
2) Vanilla: add vanilla essence to taste.
3) Lemon or orange: add lemon rind or orange rind to taste.
4) Coffee: add 1-2 tbsp instant coffee powder. Or combine with cocoa powder, ground cardamon or coffee liqueur.
5) Cinnamon & apple: add 1-2 tsp cinnamon powder and one finely diced apple to the batter. This will take a bit longer to bake!

THE COOK

Karin Marty
Zurich, Switzerland

Oceania Product Manager:
Travelhouse

METHOD

Preparation

Pre-heat oven at 180° C. Line your cupcake pan with paper cases.

The Batter

Combine butter, sugar, flour, baking powder, milk and egg in a small bowl with an electric mixer on medium speed until it's smooth and a light colour. Add flavouring / extra Ingredients of your choice; mix well. Divide mixture evenly among cupcake cases.

The Cooking

Bake for 15-20 minutes on the oven's middle rack. Do the toothpick test to ensure they're done.

DESERT STONES

Make 12

INGREDIENTS

100 g sultanas
2 eggs
100 g sugar
100 g butter
1 packet of pastry yeast
350 g flour
Corn flakes
50 g chocolate chips
Powdered sugar

TIP
For extra flavour add 1 tsp of grappa, or your favourite liqueur, to the soaking sultanas.

THE COOK

Michela Aldegheri
Verona, Italy

Manager Director:
Fiji Time Viaggi

METHOD

Preparation
Soak the sultanas in warm water for 15 minutes. Preheat the oven to 180° C.

The Mixture
In a bowl, beat 2 eggs with sugar and softened butter. Combine with yeast and flour.
Mix in the sultanas and chocolate chips. Using your hands, roll mixture into heaped-teaspoon-sized balls and roll each one in corn flakes.

The Cooking
Cook for 20 minutes.

The Finale
Add powdered sugar.

MANGO PARFAIT

Makes 12

INGREDIENTS

360 ml mango purée
440 g castor sugar
120 g butter
6 eggs yolks
100 ml lemon juice
700 ml thickened cream

Berry Sauce

200 g raspberries or mixed berries
2 tbsp honey
1 tbsp Grand Marnier
1 tbsp lime juice

THE COOK

Hamish N Isabella
Cooktown, Australia

Owner:
Mungumby Lodge

METHOD

Preparation

Combine sugar, butter, eggs yolks and lemon juice in a small bowl over pan of simmering water. Beat with electric mixer for 15 minutes or until slightly thickened. Remove from heat and beat for another 5 minutes or until mixture is thick & cool. Transfer mixture to large bowl, fold in whipped cream in 2 batches. Fold in the mango purée. Transfer into a bread tin, cover with plastic wrap. Freeze for at least 12 hours.

The Sauce Finale

Combine the berries, honey, Grand Marnier and lime juice.
Remove the frozen parfait from the tin and slice into serves.
Dress with the berry sauce.

PAVLOVA CAKE

Serves 4-6

INGREDIENTS

6 large eggs
2 cups of caster sugar
1.5 tsp vanilla essence
1.5 tsp white vinegar
600 ml whipping cream
Fresh Fruits (your choice dependant on season):
mango, kiwi fruit, passionfruit, strawberries,
other berries, banana

THE COOK

Deborah Carr
Perth, Australia
Chair:
Rottnest Island
Chamber of Commerce
WA Branch Manager
ATEC

METHOD

Preparation
Separate whites of six eggs. Cover a baking tray with greaseproof paper. Slice your fruits
and combine with passionfruit pulp, and put in fridge. Preheat oven to 150° C.

The Meringue
In a bowl beat 6 egg whites until white peaks appear. It's important they're quite stiff.
Slowly add caster sugar, then fold in vinegar and vanilla essence. Pipe or pile the mixture onto
baking tray. Bake for 45 minutes, then turn heat off and leave in oven for at least one hour.

The Finale
Place your Pavlova meringue pile on your serving dish.
Whip the cream with 1 tbsp of caster sugar.
Dress your Pavlova in alternating layers of fruit and cream.
Enjoy.

RASPBERRY AND LIME CHEESECAKE

Serves 4-6

INGREDIENTS

220 g macadamia nuts
180 g raw sugar
150 g plain flour
40 g butter
2 limes
500 g cream cheese
500 g cream
250 g raspberries

THE COOK

Gill Parssey
Hobart, Australia
Admin:
Wukalina Walk

METHOD

Preparation
Grate rind of 1 lime. Extract juice of both limes. Preheat oven to 180° C.

The Cooking
Use a blender to mix macadamia nuts and 80 g of sugar. Add flour and butter and mix again.
Press this batter into base of a 28-cm springform pan. Bake for 20 minutes or until base is golden.
Allow to cool. In the meantime, combine lime rind and 100 g of sugar and blend for 20 seconds.
Blend in lime juice and cream cheese; then add cream and mix again. Finally add raspberries
to the mixture and fold in gently with a spatula.

The Finale
Pour mixture over macadamia base in the pan and refrigerate for around 4 hours.
Garnish with lime zest and a spread of raspberries.

FAMOUS 3 INGREDIENT FRUIT CAKE

Serves 6-8

INGREDIENTS

6 cups of dried mixed fruit
600 ml black tea (see Tips)
265 g self-raising flour

TIPS

1) You can add nuts, and glace cherries to the fruit mix.
2) For flavour variety you can replace the black tea with iced coffee, chocolate milk, fruit juice.. You can also add a splash of brandy, whiskey, dark rum or port.
3) The cake can be stored for up to a month in an airtight container.

THE COOK

Judith North
Gold Coast, Australia
UK/Europe Sales:
Baillie Lodges

METHOD

Preparation
Grease and line a 23 cm cake tin with baking paper. Preheat oven to 160° C (fan-forced) or 175° C (conventional).

The Batter
Combine dried mixed fruit in a large bowl with black tea (or see Tips). Cover with plastic wrap and place into fridge overnight. When ready, add self-raising flour to fruity tea, and mix well. Pour batter into prepared cake tin.

The Cooking
Bake for 1 hour or until cake feels firm in the middle, and a skewer comes out with a few moist crumbs on it. Cool cake in tin before removing.

TIRAMISÙ

Serves 4-6

INGREDIENTS

4 eggs
80 g sugar
500 g mascarpone
250 g savoiardi biscuits (lady fingers)
Black coffee
Cocoa powder

THE COOK

Luca Dal Cookie
Genova, Italy

Scientist

METHOD

Preparation
Make a large cup of coffee. Allow to cool. Separate yolks and whites of 4 eggs. Whisk together
40 g of sugar and yolks until mixture becomes dense. Add mascarpone in small quantities
and keep whisking until smooth and creamy.
In a separate bowl, whisk egg whites for about
90 seconds. Gradually add 40 g of sugar and keep whisking briskly until mixture has peaks
and is 'fluffy like a clouds'.
Using a spoon, slowly incorporate the mascarpone mixture into egg whites, mixing from the bottom to the top until well blended. Briefly dip savoiardi biscuits
in coffee. Cover bottom of a tray or serving dish with the biscuits. Cover the first layer with
mascarpone cream. Add another layer of coffee-dipped biscuits then cover with the rest
of cream. Set tiramisù in the fridge for 10 to 12 hours.

The Finale
When you're ready to serve, dust the top with cocoa powder.

VEGAN CHOCOLATE COOKIES

Make 12

INGREDIENTS

Plain flour
Baking powder
Baking soda
Salt
190 g dark chocolate buttons
(dairy-free if vegan is a must)
110 g brown sugar
100 g cane or raw sugar
110 g vegetable oil
75 ml water
Sea salt

THE COOK

Sebastian Topet
Melbourne, Australia

Owner:
Oceania Tours & Safaris

METHOD

Preparation
Stir oil, water and sugars together in a good-sized bowl. Mix in 250 g of flour, 0.75 tsp of baking soda, 1 tsp of baking powder and a pinch of salt. Add dark chocolate buttons.
Cover and leave in fridge for 24 hours. Spoon out mixture and roll into 65 g balls.
Put in freezer for 10 minutes. Sprinkle with some sea salt.
Bake at 180° C for 13 minutes.

The Finale
Serve with your favourite beverage.

APPLE CALVADOS CAKE

Serves 4-6

INGREDIENTS

310 g caster sugar
6 Granny Smith apples
40 g calvados (apple brandy)
120 g butter
2 eggs
128 g self-raising flour

TIP
If you can't get Calvados, use brandy, cognac or, better still, Armagnac.

THE COOK

Andrew Dwyer
Jamieson, Australia

Owner:
Diamantina Touring Company

METHOD

Preparation
Peel, core and cut apples into lengths. Butter a cake tin. Preheat oven to 180° C (350° F).

The Cooking
Put 200 g of sugar in a heavy-based frying pan and slowly melt it over a low heat for 6–8 minutes. Stir at the edges as it begins to caramelise. Add apples and deglaze the pan with Calvados. Continue to cook a further 6–8 minutes until apples are caramelised and cooked through.
Tip fruit into the base of cake tin.
Cream butter with remaining sugar until light and fluffy.
Add eggs one at a time, beating well after each addition.
Gently fold in flour, then pour mixture over apples.
Bake for 35 minutes, or until a skewer inserted into cake comes out clean.

APÉRITIFS
AND DRINKS

TOOTY FRUITY COCKTAIL

Serves 2

INGREDIENTS

30 ml Cointreau
60 ml Midori
30 ml peach schnapps
30 ml Malibu
60 ml orange juice
30 ml cranberry juice
Large jug of ice
Strawberries

TIP
Why not use Martin's home-made pear schnapps!

THE COOK

Paul Cooper
Phillip Island,
Australia

Marketing Manager:
Sydney Melbourne
Touring

METHOD

Preparation
Fill a cocktail shaker with ice. Add all liquid ingredients. Shake vigorously.
Fill a highball glass with ice. Poor cocktail mix though a strainer.

The Finale
Garnish with strawberries. Add stirrer and paper straw. Serve and enjoy slowly.

PEAR SCHNAPPS

Serves 2

INGREDIENTS

3 pears
4 cinnamon sticks
Half a stick of vanilla
2 tsp coriander seeds
8 1/2 tbsp sugar
1 litre vodka
A jar large enough to take all the ingredients

THE COOK

Martin Dahl Jespersen
Oslo, Denmark

Director, Product and Business Development:
Australiareiser

METHOD

Preparation

Rinse pears and cut them into small cubes. Put chopped pears, cinnamon sticks, vanilla bean and coriander seeds into your large jar. Pour in the vodka, pop on lid and give it a good shake. Place your jar on a windowsill or other sunny spot for one week.

Open, add sugar, replace lid and place jar in a cool dark cupboard for another three weeks. Give your mixture a shake every day or so.

After three weeks in the dark, remove pears and spices, strain liquid through a sieve until mixture is clear.

Pour your schnapps into a sterilised bottle and rest for another couple of weeks.

The Finale

Your pear schnapps is best drunk ice cold.

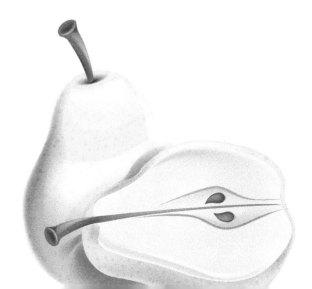

ACKNOWLEDGEMENTS

This book has been a labour of love. Many people, many hours.
Translations, conversions, timezones, Covid-19.
Teamwork. Thank you.

Roberto Chiesa: Conception and chief organiser
Paul Cooper: Project coordination
Adam Fletcher: Designer
Lindy Cameron: Publisher

A special thank you to:

Carmen Laurella, Diana Jaquillard, Morena Parati, Susanne Stellberg

THANK YOU

To all our Facebook group members of the travel industry and beyond,
a very special thank you for your passion, support, dedication and friendship:

Adam Sands
Adelene Cheah
Alan Dean
Alberto Gorgone
Alberto Panni
Alessandro Santambrogio
Alessia Franceschini
Alexandra Brunet
Alisi Lutu
Allen Brooker
Alva Hemming
Ambrogio Giacometti
Amy Sullivan
Andrea Baumann
Andreas Schunck
Andrew Dwyer
Andrew Johnston
Andrew Saunders
Andrew Woodcock
Andy Lehmann
Angela Marini
Angela Ostlind
Angelique Fransen
Angie Colombo
Angie Sayer Reidy
Anna Pezzi
Annalena Nordic Cocchi
Annalisa Anichini
Annalisa Turturiello
Annamaria Veroni
Annette Kegel
Annie Henry-Kerr
Antonella Valerio
Antonio Agnese
Antonio De Santis
Aristide Maina
Arty Holly
Astrid Weissenfeldt
Aurélia Devilliers-Fezay
Bal Naidu
Barbara Benedetti
Barbara Mauro

Barbara Monti
Beatrice Caretta
Belinda Hill
Ben Woodward
Bettina Kramer
Birgit Bourne
Birgit Sviontek
Birthe Kanzler
Bob Woodward
Brad Crooks
Bridget Lawton
Britta Henning
Bruce White
Bryan Arnicar
Bryce Earwaker
Camilla Dalponte
Carla Piazza
Carla Rocchi
Carmen Laurella
Carmen White
Caroline Densley
Carsten Vesper
Cecilia Leoni
Cherie Glare
Chris Martin
Christiane Empter Zanotti
Christine Klein
Christine Weber
Claire Chamberlain
Claire Rossi
Claudia Barbieri
Claudia Diana
Claudia Gnemmi
Claudia Somma
Claudio Borgioli
Claudio Del Bianco
Conny Shooter
Consuelo Gamba
Conta Francesco
Craig Smith
Craig Wickham
Cristina Apuani

Cristina Bernasconi
Cristina Piccinotti
Cristina Stevan
Daniel Galassi
Daniela Migli
Daniela Tagliaretti
Daniele Da-Rin
Daniele Landolina
Daniele Pizzimenti
Danielle Andreuzzi
David O'Malley
Debbie Lewis
Debbie Mark Ferguson
Deborah Carr
Denise Deveney
Denise von Wald
Diana Davidson
Diana Jaquillard
Diane Colton
Diané Ranck
Donatella Daniela Acquati
Donatella Marcocci
Drew Hamilton
Duncan Morris
Elena Barassi
Elena Paracchi
Eleonora Gramaglia
Elisa Bertero
Elisa Olivi
Elisabetta Rullo
Ellen Bousfield
Emanuela Goggia
Emma Dixon,Emma Kim
Emmer Guerra
Enrica Bighiani
Enrico Colombo
Erica Apo
Eva Huber
Eva Seller
Federica Bellinazzi
Federica Binda
Felicity Brown

THANK YOU

continued...

Feng Tam
Fiorino Fiorini
Francesca Ferrari
Francesca Petracca
Gabby Ritter
Gabriele Picco
Gabriella Giachino
Gabriella Pennestrì
Gabriella Repetto
Gabriella Tuatagaloa
Gaby Robinson
Garatti Milena
Gerard Carnot
German Diethei
Gianfranco Faglia
Gianluca Giua
Gill Parssey
Gina Beacom
Giorgia Guadagni
Giorgio Domini
Giovanni Callina
Giuliana Arras
Giulio Checchi
Glenn Sweet
Greta Bal
Hamish N Isabella
Igor TheBoss Simonaio
Ilaria Pess
Inga Afheldt
Inka Van Baal
Isabella Radaelli
Jack Waterfront
Jackie Charlton
Jaime Correa Acevedo
James Dixon
James McCann
Jasmine Baker
Jeannie Armstrong
Jeff Adam
Jeff Aquilina
Jeff Cameron-Smith
Jessica Oliviero
Jill Palise
Joanne Skinner

John Haymes
John Pugsley
Jonas Davidsson
Judith North
Jula Rohrbacher
Julia Kanzso
Julie Telford
Julie Weber
Kai Oz Ostermann
Kaltovea Kalfabun
Karen Dempster
Karen Fraser
Karen Holloway
Karen Priest
Karin Marty
Kate McCann
Katherine Droga
Katherine Reid
Kathy Graham
Katie Hill
Katja Bockwinkel
Kerry Miller
Kleon Howe
Kolora N Anthony Mason
Kristi-Anne O'Brien
Laura Dominici
Laura Franguelli
Laura Lavatelli
Laura Oliveri
Laura Puccinelli
Laura Rivoltella
Laura Testa
Laurence Meccoli
Lea Faccarello
Lee Davidson
Leonardo Ghidetti
Linda Honey
Lisa Albini
Lisa Taylor
Liz Martin
Louise Scott
Louise Terry
Luca Dalponte
Luca Fabrizio de Amicis

Luciana Bolgia
Luigi Leone
Lusiana Tabua Saukitoga
Lyn Tuit
Lynda Schumacher
Lynne Mischewski
Mandy Brown
Manny Papadoulis
Manu Fox
Manuela Borsotti
Marc A. Lambert
Marco Dal Zotto
Marcus Falconer
Margaret Soh
Margret Stornebrink
Maria Ida Perugini
Maria Teresa Omede
Mariateresa Truncellito
Mariella Cirasole
Marina Casarotto
Marina Firrao
Marina Lanza
Mark Badland
Mark Beech
Mark Skinner
Mary Carroll
Mary Retzler
Maryanne Jacques
Massimiliano Lenzi
Massimo Bonifazi
Matilde De Simone
Matt Jones
Melanie Grevis-James
Melissa Wiltshire
Mia Daskalu-Johnson
Mia Hezi
Mia Osterberg
Michael Healy
Michela Aldegheri
Michela Longo
Michela Massa
Michelle Papas
Mirco Solfanelli
Mirela Cristina Murariu

THANK YOU

continued...

MIrella Castagna
Moka Monica Penny
Monia Lancerotto
Morag Ginger Ritchie
Morena Parati
Nancy Lowe
Naomi An Chris Chambers
Natalie Rose
Neville Poelina
Nick Olò
Nicole Maerten
Nicole Mitchell
Nicole Passarelli
Nicoletta Mangolini
Norman Tassin
Ombretta Pepe
Ornella D'alessio
Orsola Lalatta
Paige Myles
Paola Arras
Paola Broggini
Parodi Pietro
Patrizia Brunod
Patrizia Martelli
Paul Cooper
Pauline Wagner-Carden
Penny Rafferty
Peter Arp
Petra Steinig
Petrel van Bronkhorst
Pia Krechel
Pietro Tarallo
Pola la Mattina
Ralph Jackson
Regina Twiss
Rhett Lego
Ricarda Jeromin
Richard Doyle
Rick Thomas
Roberta Bertazza Costantini
Roberta Busolo
Roberta Carollo
Roberta Poli
Roberta Rho

Roberto Rovera
Robyn Maher
Robyn Quinlan
Rodney Twiss
Ron Livingston
Rosa Valcarenghi
Rosalind Harries
Rudi Francken
Sab Lord
Sabina Mazzi
Sabina Tognon
Sabine Schamburger
Sabrina Nicolosi
Sabrina Sicura
Sally Holyer
Salome Lewa
Salvatore Busardo
Sandra Etter
Sandra Feustel
Sandra Lange
Ina Becker
Sara Avigo
Sara Ruvutuso
Sara Sandri
Sebastian Topet
Sebastien Cros
Shane O'Reilly
Sheena Walshaw
Shelagh Murphy
Shirley Dodt
Silvia Bassanetti
Silvia Bossini
Silvia Catucci
Silvia Druetto
Silvia Farano
Silvia Meletti
Silvia Mengali
Silvia Vizzoni
Simona la Salandra
Simona Pelicani
Simona Seghetti
Simona Silva
Slava Atkins
Sonia Beckwith

Sonia Rizzo
Sonja Sarlin
Steen Grosen Andersen
Stella Dielhenn
Stephanie Lang
Stephanie Siebert
Steven Gargano
Steven Vervaeke
Suada Rrapaj
Susan Crockford
Susanne Larsson
Susanne Miller
Susanne Ritzen Österberg
Susanne Stellberg
Susie De Carteret
Suzann Eckert von Hagen
Sven Dijkstra
Swee Wah
Sylvia Zengerer
Tania Jacobs
Tara Bennett
Teresa Scacchi
Tonia Home
Tony Howell
Valdis Dūnis
Valentina Costa
Valentini Damariva
Victoria Matterson
Vincenza Pearce
Warrick Welsh
Wendy Besoo
Wendy Morris
Wilma Panni
Xavier Urpí Gispert
Ziga Kmetic
Roberto Chiesa

Lightning Source UK Ltd.
Milton Keynes UK
UKHW050740090223
416597UK00002B/7